Fitzgerald-Wilson-Hemingway

Fitzgerald-Wilson-Hemingway
Language and Experience

Ronald Berman

THE UNIVERSITY OF ALABAMA PRESS
Tuscaloosa and London

Copyright © 2003
THE UNIVERSITY OF ALABAMA PRESS
Tuscaloosa, Alabama 35487-0380
All rights reserved
Manufactured in the United States of America

Typeface: Fairfield Light and Parisian

∞

The paper on which this book is printed meets the minimum requirements of American National Standard for Information Science–Permanence of Paper for Printed Library Materials, ANSI Z39.48-1984.

Library of Congress Cataloging-in-Publication Data

Berman, Ronald.
Fitzgerald-Wilson-Hemingway : language and experience / Ronald Berman.
p. cm.
Includes index.
ISBN 0-8173-1278-1 (alk. paper)
1. Fitzgerald, F. Scott (Francis Scott), 1896–1940—Criticism and interpretation—History. 2. Hemingway, Ernest, 1899–1961—Criticism and interpretation—History. 3. American fiction—20th century—History and criticism—Theory, etc. 4. Fitzgerald, F. Scott (Francis Scott), 1896–1940—Language. 5. Wilson, Edmund, 1895–1972—Knowledge—Literature. 6. Criticism—United States—History—20th century. 7. Hemingway, Ernest, 1899–1961—Language. I. Title.

PS3511.I9 Z55775 2003
810.9'0052—dc21
2002015041

British Library Cataloguing-in-Publication Data available

A shorter version of chapter 2, "America in Fitzgerald," appeared in the *Journal of Aesthetic Education* 36, no. 2 (summer 2002): 38–51. Printed with permission. The version published here contains new material.

For Barbara and our family

CONTENTS

	Introduction	1
1	The Last Romantic Critic	9
2	America in Fitzgerald	25
3	Edmund Wilson and Alfred North Whitehead	42
4	Reality's Thickness	58
5	Hemingway's Plain Language	75
6	Hemingway's Limits	86
	Notes	101
	Index	119

Fitzgerald-Wilson-Hemingway

Introduction

We get a sense of immediacy from novels of the twenties. However, we are now further from *The Great Gatsby* and *The Sun Also Rises* than Lionel Trilling was from the late work of Henry James at the time of *The Liberal Imagination*. The twenties are rapidly receding. We need to do a certain amount of rediscovery, to examine terms that were in use then that mean something else now. Writers of the twenties dealt with concepts of experience, perception, and reality. They had ideas about what language could do and what literature might be. But we have elided meanings, and we assume that F. Scott Fitzgerald was a romantic whose themes were love and the American dream; that Edmund Wilson's criticism was based on common sense without much theory; that Hemingway succeeded in capturing experience by simplifying language, making it ever more precise. The facts are broader. Fitzgerald was a romantic but also a close student of romanticism, which is something different. Wilson was much concerned with writing as one of the "outcomes of science."[1] He was seriously interested in the transubstantiation of facts (the phrase comes from John Dewey) by language. Hemingway's best work is not a result of objectifying experience but rests, I think, on the uneasy awareness of its resistance to language.

From 1919 on, Fitzgerald's reviews, essays, and interviews displayed ideas about language. They were done in the absence of contemporary literary criticism—H. L. Mencken was useful in small doses, but Fitzgerald had justifiable contempt for the rest. He was well informed on romantic theory, applying it ruthlessly to his own writing and to the work of other novelists. Books now coming into play remind us that he was an active critic.[2] His 1929 letter to John Peale Bishop about basing novels on any "philosophical system" indicates acquaintance, however partial, with both subjects.[3] The letter is a stinging reminder of Fitzgerald's capacity for textual detail—as is the concurrent letter to Hemingway identifying good and bad points of A Farewell to Arms.

Fitzgerald had expectations about language and ideas. He recognized the arguments of romanticism and brought them up-to-date. We don't want to think of him as being himself "romantic" about the character, situation, or fate of Jay Gatsby. He applied doctrine developed by Coleridge, Keats, and Wordsworth. Life was short and one accepted that. It needed meaning—something literature supplied. But the statement of meaning was difficult, and in order to ascertain it, certain patterns of experience needed to be understood: the inexorable passage of time and life that compelled existence to define itself; the universal desire to repeat experience; the great constant of subjectivity. These things were also philosophical issues of the twenties: the idea of repeating early experience, for example, underlay Walter Lippmann's fairly hardheaded analysis of political idealism.[4]

While Fitzgerald often used the term "romantic" in his critical writing, it rarely applied to sensibility, sensation, or emotion. It did mean heightened perception of what he described as exactness of detail. His own diction was simple, representing an attempt to renew the significance of familiar things. In the margin of the typescript of A Farewell to Arms, he wrote about the reunion of Frederic Henry and Catherine at Stresa: "This is one of the most beautiful pages in all English literature." Here is the passage he had in mind: "If people bring so much courage to this world the world has to kill them to break them, so of course it kills them."[5] It seems unremarkable, monosyllabic, repetitive. But it puts the pressure on words themselves. It may be that Hemingway's simplified language resonated in some special way, a way that the following passage conveys. Both writers base their attack on meaning on the conception—one should say the shock—of renewed familiarity: "Michaelis and this man reached her first but when they had torn open her shirtwaist still damp with perspiration they saw that her left breast was swinging loose like a flap and there was no need to listen for the heart beneath. The mouth was wide open and ripped at the corners as though she had choked a little in giving up the tremendous vitality she had stored so long."[6] The intellectual momentum is extraordinary, cutting from short bursts of action to longer, more conceptual ideas that impose—and also severely contain—meaning. Because nothing is sacred, the passage conjoins haberdashery and hardware and dying without a touch of metaphysics. There is no interpretation (Daisy's car swerves away "tragically," distanced both as object and conception), so the excluded is as meaningful as the included. Fitzgerald too had a fairly hard-edged idea of actual circumstance and of its discorrelation from meanings.

Fitzgerald's novels, which are centrally about the creation of American identity, are not clarified by politics alone. The idea of "America" was connected to and modified by other terms such as "rise," "fall," and "civilization." The last of these terms—it is the great catch phrase of the decade—is on the small but crowded mind of Tom Buchanan. He is attuned to ideas that, at the end of their diaspora from William James and Walter Lippmann, alight finally on the *Saturday Evening Post*. They have to do with the idea of progress, disguised in the Jazz Age as success. When Babbitt speechifies about America to the realtors of Zenith, his subject seems at first out of place: "In other countries, art and literature are left to a lot of shabby bums living in attics and feeding on booze and spaghetti, but in America the successful writer or picture-painter is indistinguishable from any other decent business man."[7] But the allusion makes sense; even in Zenith, "civilization" now is American. (We glory in the fact that of the four hundred or so colors known to humanity, "more than one-third are used in women's stockings."[8]) The "rise" of American civilization was one of the ideas in place during the twenties. Fitzgerald was on the other side of that idea. His characters live out the disputed issues of Americanism, immigration, and the new, uneasy relationship of province and metropolis. But they understand the difference between promise and embodiment.

Fitzgerald shared convictions that had for some time been aired by William James, Walter Lippmann, and George Santayana. The same is true of Edmund Wilson. Wilson, however, was a more rigorous thinker, and he cast a wider net. Like Fitzgerald, he began to think about writing from the viewpoint of romanticism. In order to find some historical room for modernism, Wilson bypassed Victorian poetry, finding what he needed in Wordsworth and Shelley. Both his fiction and criticism in the late twenties make the point that romanticism provided the intellectual underpinning for modernism. He did not get that idea from literary histories; it came from Alfred North Whitehead's *Science and the Modern World* (1925) and his essays on symbolic logic.

Whitehead influenced Wilson profoundly, to the point of appearing as a character, the charismatic Professor Grosbeake, in *I Thought of Daisy*. Whitehead had worked out a theory of the translation of phenomena to language, a process that needed a good deal more than the words and ideas available to science. In fact, *Science and the Modern World* argued that science had to understand the larger language available to poetry. The central issue was that Wordsworthian poetry "expresses the concrete facts of our apprehension." This goes further than acknowledging that such poetry (in this case he refers to Shelley) symbolizes "joy," "peace," and "illumination." So far as Whitehead was concerned, we begin to understand through romanticism the description of the inorganic, the functioning of organisms, and "the full content of our perceptual experience."[9]

Wilson was able to write about symbolism and modernist poetry because of Whitehead's 1927 lectures on symbolic logic. Whitehead stated several major points: first among them, that "perception of the external world" depends upon its presentation; second, that there are "symbolic references" in almost every perceived thing or quantity. The latter, more complex than it looks, involves the idea that our own experience is "relational." Each "actual physical organism enters into the make-up of its contemporaries."[10] Because of this input from Whitehead, *I Thought of Daisy* shares some of the critical importance of *Axel's Castle*. It follows Whitehead's work on poetry, notably his idea of "presentational immediacy." The phrase (originally Wordsworth's) means, for both Whitehead and Wilson, the ability to wield language complex enough to describe phenomena. One of Whitehead's most important points is that concrete, individual things, organic or not, become related to, even part of the conceiving mind. A problem is raised because, as we see in the cases of William James, Whitehead, and Wilson, this leads to the mystical side of romanticism.

On the scientific side, Whitehead seems to have formulated Wilson's systematic perception. Whitehead repeatedly stressed the importance of "colour" and "substance." These terms show up consistently in the symbolic logic essays, referring to the ways in which we react to things outside ourselves. They have a long history, and Whitehead himself seems to have found them in romantic poetry. In any case, he invariably describes the operation of light when he characterizes phenomena. It is as if he provided Wilson with a map: the governing idiom of the second (and most important) part of *I Thought of Daisy* describes ambient, reflected, and refracted light in immense detail. Santayana, a good representative of the turn-of-century generation, wrote that "the primacy of sight in our perception . . . makes light the natural symbol of knowledge." It is, he continued, "a logically natural link between the metaphysical and the actual."[11]

From the consideration of this sector of ideas, Wilson began to think in terms of their equivalents. Whitehead had not been alone in requiring a language complex enough to do justice to perception; both William James and John Dewey had argued at length about the form such language should take. One of the most interesting things about the public philosophy was its sympathy for literature. To go through the pages of James and Dewey, to say nothing of Josiah Royce, Lippmann, Santayana, and James's disciple Horace M. Kallen, is to be immersed in nineteenth-century poetry and fiction. In one burst of commentary on William James, Royce invokes Coleridge, Dostoevsky, Kipling, Shakespeare, and the Brownings. In part, philosophical allusion to literature was a way of finding exempla for human behavior; this allusion is morally rather than critically intense. But an important part of such allusion, especially in James, Whitehead, and Dewey, was directed at the capacity of literature to reveal reality. "Reality" was an important term in the twenties, as was "literature," which meant more than art or story.

We can get some sense of what literature meant by reading Walter Lippmann on Upton Sinclair. Lippmann loathes early-twentieth-century fiction, calling it lazy, slack, timid, sentimental, untrue. The heart of the matter, to Lippmann, is that fiction is *philosophically* untrue. Its unconvincing characters cannot illuminate the issues of the real world, and "you cannot send a man to American literature so that he may enrich his experience and deepen his understanding." In this regard, Lippmann comes close to issues that mattered to Edmund Wilson and to Hemingway, especially the central issue of stating "concrete passions and actual sensations."[12] It was a small step from there to the examination of what exactly constituted perception, consciousness, and experience. Dewey, who dominated philosophy in the twenties, argued that art best understood consciousness. He stated, in fact, that "poetry, the drama, the novel, are proofs that the problem of presentation is not insoluble."[13] It could reasonably be put that he framed philosophical analysis in novelistic terms. One of his 1929 essays on experience assesses literature as epistemology: "a comment on nature and life in the interest of a more intense and just appreciation of the meanings present in experience."[14] A second essay written in the same year describes experience in terms of the plots of fiction: "*what* men do and suffer, *what* they strive for, love, believe and endure, and also *how* men act and are acted upon, the ways in which they do and suffer, desire and enjoy, see, believe, imagine—in short, processes of *experiencing*."[15] Whitehead has the same habit of mind.

The emphasis, however, should be put on knowing. Both Edmund Wilson and Lionel Trilling referred themselves to ideas of Dewey and of William James; both were intensely concerned with the idea of "reality's thickness," a Jamesian phrase invoked by Trilling to account for the *resistance* of experience to its formulation. In terms of phenomenology, it was to be understood that reality quickly exhausted the modes of discerning it. There was, in short, a realm of experience beyond the powers of perception and of articulation. For Trilling especially, this meant that there was a boundary for critical ideas. There could be no possible point to evolving a scheme insufficient to its elements. One understood that reality was many layered and could not be captured except in some partial way. Trilling transferred the idea to social thought, which may be why he is so much out of favor today. He argued that the equipment of liberalism was insufficient to perceive or understand the complex nature of experience. His remarkable essay on Hemingway stated that when "fine social feelings" were directed at literature, when noble sentiments and optimism determined literary attitudes, and when there was impatience with irony and indirection, literature could no longer serve as a public art. But the issue was always Jamesian: the thickness of reality resisted not only perception but the cathexis of idealism.[16] The point so important to Trilling had been taken up by Lippmann, who had this to say about the problem of "reality" in Upton Sinclair: "The power to drive home brutal facts—raw, bloody, screaming facts—made 'The Jungle' great. But when in 'The Metropolis' he came to expose the vices of the rich, he had to deal with subtler, quiet things: with manners, with snobbishness, idleness of soul, with evils that are often attractive. He hated them as intensely as he had hated poisoned meat. He hated them so intensely that he hardly saw them. 'High Society' couldn't see the reality, because of the wildness of Mr. Sinclair's emotions about it, and the world went on unimpressed."[17] Trilling reworked this argument around the "actuality of personal life" that Fitzgerald had represented in his fiction. He used the same comparison of the subtle gradation of manners among the rich.[18]

Early-twentieth-century philosophy had allocated to literature the depiction of reality, actuality, and experience. Lippmann thought it the natural province of a good novelist to show the world as it was; Santayana agreed that "language has its function of expressing experience with exactness"; Bertrand Russell assumed "that a certain sentence should assert a certain fact."[19] But Hemingway had less confidence in the powers of language. We need to take seriously Rinaldi's remark in *A Farewell to Arms* that "I know many things I can't say" because it is a Hemingway rubric. There were, Jake Barnes says of his *afición*, "no set questions that could bring it out." And Brett Ashley is Bergsonian by temperament, knowing that words not only fail to describe but actually turn against their subject. In *The Sun Also Rises* silence is an intellectual and moral value. Dialogue rejects what Jake Barnes and Brett Ashley often call "talk." Talking about things doesn't resolve anything, much less does it accomplish the by-now mythological end of understanding reality. As Mike says of that particular issue, "I'm not one of you literary chaps. . . . I'm not clever." That is to say, reality is their line of work, but its statement is duplicitous.

"A Clean, Well-Lighted Place" understands the large investment of philosophical language in the depiction, uncovering, and understanding of reality. Wilson and Whitehead wrote endlessly about the primacy of light because it is (I am using Santayana's phrase once again) "the natural symbol of knowledge." But the story is situated phenomenologically and metaphorically in darkness. What we take to be setting is symbol. The extraordinary descriptions of substance and quantity that begin the story—line, movement, light, shade, dimensionality, solidity of placement, corporeality—depict reality *as if description were explanation.* But even the passage of time is false reassurance that we are getting somewhere. The story displays all of the counters of reality, invites the conclusion that by perceiving the scene with such clarity we can unwind it. The opening is a parable of the work assigned by philosophy to literature.

But it is a scene without an interpretation. Both waiters fail entirely to penetrate the meaning of the old man—the younger waiter because he is a kind of sump of our own worldly wisdom, the older waiter because the kind of ideas needed to understand things are no longer available in 1932. I don't think it an exaggeration to say that this story has political overtones, because if nothing avails, politics can't be exempt. The well-policed setting implies the hostile presence of the state, and the ideas diffused by the younger waiter imply the way it thinks. The story closes off a generation of inquiry into the understanding of life by literature. We don't understand it, and language works mainly to prevent the understanding of it. The story has its effect because it is a coda.

I concentrate on this story and on *The Sun Also Rises* because they react so strongly against the idea that language is definitive. They follow Wittgenstein, not Dewey. The dialogues of the novel will allude to the difficulty of following one's own consciousness, and to the greater difficulty of communicating the answerable. The dialogues of the story end in blind alleys of inquiry. In certain ways these two works of fiction shadow the development of thought about language and literature. They have memorable characters with enormous, misplaced confidence in denotation and explanation. Robert Cohn and the younger waiter in the short story have obdurate faith in fake ideas. But the others, less easily formulated, are indirect, usually without much confidence (itself an important term in "A Clean, Well-Lighted Place") in the ability to undo any of the layers of reality's thickness.

1

The Last Romantic Critic

In any discussion of romanticism the number of respondents will equal the number of definitions proposed. It is sobering to read Isaiah Berlin's "In Search of a Definition," the first of his Mellon Lectures on romanticism, in which he goes over ground covered by A. O. Lovejoy, adding his own thoughts on its thematic elements of youth, exuberance, the natural, the morbid, decadence, radiance, turbulence, darkness, the strange, the weird, the familiar, the antique, novelty, desire to live in the moment, rejection of knowledge, the love of innocence, timelessness, creativity, will, dandyism, art, and primitivism.[1] I have condensed liberally; the above is a fraction of what Lovejoy and Berlin respectively listed.

In regard to Fitzgerald a certain amount of defining needs to be done. His romanticism takes specific tactical form, extending images past reality and past the capabilities of realism; he creates an extraordinary sense of the spirit of place; and he reminds us of emotional powers not easily understood by (mere) rationality.[2] He is rightly linked to Keats, whose verses "stick in your memory."[3] But Fitzgerald's romanticism went against the national grain. Simply to assert romanticism was to take part in a cultural argument loudly conducted. Romantic expectation was a theme, he recognized, not of high culture but of movies and magazines.[4]

The American tendency in literature had been to affirm or (as H. L. Mencken wrote at comic length) to avoid reality.[5] We sense the former in the grand finale to William James's *Pragmatism*. James was an extraordinary intellectual presence. But he had a Victorian conception of literature, understanding it as a guide to moral action. The last chapter of *Pragmatism* begins, remarkably, with fifty-two lines cited from Walt Whitman's long poem "To You." James then translates these lines into moral suasion: they "may mean your better possibilities phenomenally taken, or the specific redemptive effects even of your failures, upon yourself or . . . your loyalty to the possibilities of others." They set "definite activities in us at work."[6] As James and other late-Victorian critics understand the issues, poetry civilizes, gives us workable advice. Characteristically generous, James allows for many interpretations of Whitman's poem. He was himself more complex, but Victorians understood poetry in terms of the moral quality of what was said—and romanticism arrived in the twentieth century as interpreted by Victorians.

The problem was recognized by Van Wyck Brooks, who between 1915 and 1927 published a group of essays attacking late-Victorian sensibility. He took on both James and Whitman, finding in the former literary ideas that were far too simple, really only forms of poetic utilitarianism. Brooks wrote that the great pragmatists (he called them "awakeners" of the twentieth-century American mind) deserved respect, but that "they were not sufficiently poets to intensify the conception of human nature they had inherited from our tradition. Their own vein of poetry, golden in William James, silver in John Dewey, ran too thin for that." The crucial point was that they converted poetry into something else. "Assuming that the intelligence is the final court of appeal . . . all they can do, therefore, is to unfold the existing fact in themselves, and in the world about them." Referring to Emerson's utilitarian view of Shelley, Brooks sums up what a new generation of writers should know: Victorians understood poetry as public advice.[7]

The problem with "original" early-nineteenth-century romanticism was that it had been transvalued by Victorianism. Transvalued, one might say, with a vengeance: the *Shelburne Essays* of Paul Elmer More, published before and during the war years, understood romantic sensibility as social philosophy. More saw great danger in the creation of "the infinitely craving personality, the usurpation of emotion over reason, the idealization of love, the confusion of the sensuous and the spiritual, the perilous fascination that may go with the confusions." Not a good entry into *Gatsby* for the common reader. More was especially hostile to the effects of romanticism on individuality—which was raised, he said, "to a state of morbid excess"—and he hated the confusion of things finite and infinite.[8] He was joined by Irving Babbitt, whose *Rousseau and Romanticism* of 1919 famously described Keats as beauty without wisdom, and Shelley as feeling without understanding. Neither poet was, he thought, useful to Americans—their ethics were simply too confused—and they should be read only now and then for purposes of wary "recreation."[9] If we are to judge from these evaluations of artistic purpose, Victorians taught Fitzgerald's generation that romanticism should be identified with advice either good or bad directed toward some ulterior purpose.

Romanticism had become less persuasive as an intellectual mode after the propaganda of the Great War ground out thousands of posters of soldiers in shining armor and circulated the awful "epic" poetry of Henry Newbolt and W. E. Henley encouraging patriotism—and enlistment.[10] Intellectuals had little faith left in those themes of quest, chivalry, idealism, and sacrifice that inform *The Great Gatsby*.[11] In any case, after Wittgenstein, John Dewey, and Bertrand Russell had attacked politicized rhetoric in the early twenties one no longer trusted high-sounding intent.[12] Ezra Pound, T. S. Eliot, and T. E. Hulme exerted their influence in favor of a different sensibility. As Geoffrey H. Hartman puts the matter, "in the years following World War I, it became customary to see classicism and romanticism as two radically different philosophies of life, and to place modernism on the side of the antiromantic."[13]

We need only remind ourselves of Edmund Wilson's position as the decade began: If the new subjects of poetry were to be "blank buildings and slaughter-houses and factories . . . Claxon-blowing motor-cars and typewriters cracking like machine-guns, taxicabs, jazz-bands, trick electric signs, enormous hotels plastered heavily with a garish magnificence, streets and street-cars . . . the crash and grinding of the traffic . . . the whole confused and metallic junk-heap of the modern American city" then it would no longer be possible for emotions to "find expression in the forms of Milton and Shelley."[14] In the face of such attitudes, it took some determination to announce romantic purpose between the Great War and *The Great Gatsby.*

During that period, Fitzgerald produced not only novels and short stories but essays, reviews, and letters, also. He gave some notable interviews. In general, his critical work will identify his literary allegiances; compare romanticism (favorably) with realism; and introduce, recall, and elaborate romantic theory. An interview of 1923 invokes a list of literary godfathers: Henry James, Nietzsche, H. G. Wells, Shaw, Mencken, Dreiser, and Conrad. All are to be admired. But Fitzgerald understands something that Wells, Shaw, and Mencken do not: the idea of criticism has changed. Here is how the interviewer puts the matter: "F. Scott Fitzgerald, the prophet and voice of the younger American smart set, says that while Conrad's *Nostromo* is the great novel of the past fifty years, *Ulysses* by James Joyce is the great novel of the future."[15] We see the silent presence of Edmund Wilson who had shortly before this reviewed *Ulysses,* recommended it to Fitzgerald, and begun to elaborate modernism's own great tradition.[16]

Fitzgerald is consistently interested in what is happening among other writers. For example, his review of Sherwood Anderson's *Many Marriages* tries to set that novel within the intellectual context of the twenties. He raises public issues and issues of moral intention and consequence. Although self-consciously a modern, he notes that opinion about society matters very little in the business of writing. Fashionable ideas about the end of monogamy (a subject now and then on Tom Buchanan's mind) may be simply "propaganda" for intellectuals. Ever conscious of fact, Fitzgerald criticizes the failure of Anderson to measure up to the social thickness of Dreiser, Joyce, and Wells, stating that "for purpose of the book no such background as Dublin Catholicism, middlewestern morality, or London Fabianism could ever have existed."[17]

This kind of assessment is often made in Fitzgerald's short pieces, requiring us to know something about the literary scene in the generation before the twenties. But, even more emphatically, we keep being referred by his allusions to ideas that long antedate the twenties. When Fitzgerald uses the term "romantic" to analyze contemporary fiction—

and he uses the term a lot—he expects us to understand particular sources and to arrive at some sense of their modern applications.

Fitzgerald's "Public Letter to Thomas Boyd," which appeared in the *St. Paul Daily News* in the winter of 1921, reflects on the opposition between the real and the romantic. Fitzgerald admitted that fake romanticism—exemplified by novels such as Floyd Dell's *Moon-Calf*—might be entirely *too* successful. (Fitzgerald often mentioned this particular novel when he was irritated by best-seller banality. Dell became his W. H. Hudson, and the *Moon-Calf* his *Purple Land*.) The great flaw of such novels was, Fitzgerald wrote, their mindless dependence on formulaic sentimentality. How many novels about the *weltschmerz* of the privileged young could the public absorb? It was a warning to himself, and he wrote with a certain sympathy that "Dreiser would probably maintain that romanticism tends immediately to deteriorate to the Zane Grey–Rupert Hughes level, as it has in the case of Tarkington." But "the romantic side" was bound to have a great deal of support from other writers, because facts are insufficient as a basis for narrative. Reporting has no plot, cannot substitute for meaning. The interview displays a man of letters who knows how hard it is to navigate between realism and romance, and who is fully aware of the literary scene. He distrusts his audience, a theme often to be invoked. He uses the term "romantic" as if it were a synonym for insight, implying knowledge as well as feeling. Most important, it allows us to understand how facts affect our consciousness.[18] Later statements of the point will emphasize that romantic ideas are philosophical ideas, not effusions, and that they work better for fiction than other ideas propounded in the drab, unintellectual American milieu of the early twenties.

Later that year, in reviewing *Three Soldiers* by John Dos Passos, Fitzgerald again argued that the conventional audience for fiction is an adversary to its writing: "This book will not be read in the West. *Main Street* was too much of a strain. I doubt if the 'cultured' public of the Middle Border will ever again risk a serious American novel, unless it is heavily baited with romantic love. No, *Three Soldiers* will never compete with *The Sheik* or . . . Zane Grey." He knows from his own work how difficult the choice is between genuine feeling and sentiment. He then argues an issue that goes considerably beyond the literature of the early twenties: there is in good writing no "uncorrelated detail" or "clumsy juggling with huge masses of material" so characteristic of American realism.[19] The argument is central to the history of romantic thought, and Fitzgerald revives its original formulation.

Earl Wasserman has written that romantic philosophy needed "to find a significant relationship between the subjective and objective worlds." That is to say, between ideas and perceived details. Coleridge had emphasized that "the material" (unlike Fitzgerald, he means facts, not subjects) had to be governed by "the formal." Wasserman's essay concludes that "What Wordsworth, Coleridge, Keats and Shelley chose to confront more centrally and to a degree unprecedented in English literature is a nagging problem in their literary culture: How do subject and object meet in a meaningful relationship? By what means do we have a *significant* awareness of the world?"[20] Romantics disagree among themselves about what "imagination" means, but they do not disagree about the need to apply to "the external world" *some* pattern that allows us to understand it.[21] As Fitzgerald put the matter in a later review, out of muddy lakes of observation should come clear streams of ideas.[22]

Also in the fall of 1921, Fitzgerald set down one of his many observations on Europe: it is an American subgenre. What he has to say about France, England, and Italy was in the early twenties part of a national dialogue on the decline of "civilization."[23] Fitzgerald's piece contains ideas that will be repeated in his later writing and unwinds one of the grand themes of romantic history, the entropy of race and nation.

> We had been to Oxford before—after Italy we went back there arriving gorgeously at twilight when the place was fully peopled for us by the ghosts of ghosts—the characters, romantic, absurd or melancholy, of *Sinister Street, Zuleika Dobson* and *Jude the Obscure*. But something was wrong now—something that would never be right again. Here was Rome—here on the High were the shadows of the Via Appia. In how many years would our descendants approach this ruin with supercilious eyes to buy postcards from men of a short, inferior race—a race that once were Englishmen. How soon—for money follows the rich

lands and the healthy stock, and art follows begging after money. Your time will come, New York.[24]

The ruins of time will be a theme of "The Diamond as Big as the Ritz" and *The Great Gatsby*.[25] Fitzgerald's "Handle with Care," one of his confessional essays in *The Crack-Up*, suggests what the theme meant to him. This essay cites Wordsworth's line, "there had passed away a glory from the earth" from the *Immortality Ode*.[26] Such theory as there was in the early thirties had drawn connections: Hoxie Fairchild's *The Romantic Quest* (1931) observing that the passage was not merely a plangent meditation on mortality, but part of a great argument over "the dominance of man's creative will over the material world." That in itself is of enormous interest for the *Gatsby* theme of corrupted American history. But the line is written in a kind of psychological shorthand, which may be the main point, *implying the loss of authorial control and the inability to structure experience in language*.[27] To keep writing about the decay of the world was to state an essential problem of writers and subjects. We are accustomed to making the leap from subject to self with Hemingway, and need to do the same with Fitzgerald. When he talks about the end of history or of life stages he means us to extrapolate, to understand that the failure of the self has been prefigured by history. It is useful to see Fairchild's analysis of romantic subject and romantic self dated shortly before Fitzgerald's own account of his loss both of self and authorial powers in 1936. Fitzgerald's essay emphasizes that "I had become identified with the objects of my horror or compassion" and adds that the main implication is "the death of accomplishment." The conjoining of narrator and subject is, according to Marilyn Butler's useful definition, "self-reflexivity," an essential aspect of romantic poetry.[28]

Fitzgerald made some comments in a letter of late 1921 that extend his point. The passage begins with a sardonic line that has become famous among writers: "Who in hell ever respected Shelley, Whitman, Poe, O. Henry, Verlaine, Swinburne, Villon, Shakespeare ect when they were alive."[29] Isaiah Berlin has devoted a good deal of thought to this trope (the anger of art at culture has a long literary history) because it is central to romantic education, and also to a certain view of philosophy.

He makes the point that the trope of neglect matters not because artists believe it or are comforted by it but because it is true. It is also important, because pluralistic knowledge is essential for social being. Berlin reminds us that we require alternative ways of judging experience, and asserts that romanticism produces knowledge otherwise unavailable. Yet, writers have become "superfluous persons" who cannot assert themselves "against the fearful opposition offered by the philistines, the slaves, the heteronomous creatures of the society in which they live." But in this argument, which is difficult if not impossible for art to win, the *intellectual* as well as social stakes are high. The artist correctly perceives that virtually all attempts to manufacture order out of being are artificial. The powers that be (and there are many such in Fitzgerald's writing) have an interest in defining the temporary as the real and lasting, which means that the idea of order can itself be an interesting fiction. The artistic "complaint," much undervalued, is in fact a critique.[30]

Throughout the early twenties Fitzgerald continued to frame his critical writing in terms of romanticism fighting the dominance of a realist paradigm. His review of Charles Norris's *Brass* in late 1921 made a fundamental distinction: "passion" and "pain" were not qualities brought by the writer to the work but expressions of the emotions of his characters. It is difficult to overestimate the importance of the argument because it changes the notion of authorial purpose, the end of romantic writing being not for the author to express *himself* but for his characters adequately to state their experience.[31] In 1922 Fitzgerald reviewed Aldous Huxley's *Crome Yellow*, noting its "almost romantic structure" and beginning his own train of thought on metaphorical statement. This is an important essay because it begins to use a certain kind of descriptive language not available to realism. Huxley's novel offers more than a treatment of the ruins of time. *Crome Yellow* is recognizably an armature for description in the third chapter of *The Great Gatsby*:

> *Crome Yellow* is a . . . satirical novel concerning the gay doings of a house party at an English country place. . . . The book is yellow within and without. . . . A sort of yellow haze of mellow

laughter plays over it. The people are now like great awkward canaries trying to swim in saffron pools, now like bright yellow leaves blown along a rusty path under a yellow sky. . . . The satire scorns to burn deeper than a pale yellow sun, but only glints with a desperate golden mockery upon the fair hair of the strollers on the lawn; upon those caught by dawn in the towers; upon those climbing into the hearse at the last—beaten by the spirit of yellow mockery.[32]

As Eliot said, good poets steal.

Fitzgerald's May 1922 review of Shane Leslie's *The Oppidan* is about "the most romantic figure I had ever known," but by now this may no longer of itself be a significant criterion. The review has much to say about the essentials of romanticism, which do not include mysticism, sentimentality, association with Rupert Brooke, even that Catholicism that had given "the succession of days upon gray days, passing under its plaintive ritual, the romantic glamour of an adolescent dream." Nor does depiction of "the time of Shelley" guarantee artistic accomplishment. Fitzgerald's unstated point is that the romantic subject matters less than romantic strategy. He reinforced it later in the same year, stating that Peggy Boyd's *The Love Legend*, with its "lovely, ill-constructed" language, made the idea of awakening persuasive to the audience of realism.[33] It was not the subject but its statement that mattered.

There are some romantic ideas that Fitzgerald modified. In 1923, he contributed a list of "10 Best Books I Have Read" to the *Jersey City Evening Journal*. At various times in his life different titles were to occupy different places on such lists, but this one should be noted because the second book chosen was *The Philosophy of Friedrich Nietzsche*, by H. L. Mencken. Although we tend to think of him as an unreconstructed realist, Mencken transmitted some important late-romantic ideas. Some of them became part of Fitzgerald's stories, others surface in *The Great Gatsby*, others were briefly held up to the critical eye and then discarded. To look through parts of this Mencken book is to see Fitzgerald's philosophical vocabulary in the making. There is an entire chapter on "Civilization," which is a subject of immense importance in *Gatsby*'s opening, discussed (or nervously avoided) by all the main characters. So far as providing an idea about Gatsby himself, Mencken opposes what he calls "sublime egotism" to the mere conventionality of civilization. Unlike modern critics of Fitzgerald, he has no particular problem with the conception. He uses the word "gorgeous" to describe the Nietzschean hero—who does indeed in *Gatsby* have "something gorgeous about him." This is a Nietzschean characteristic, not a display of bad taste. Gatsby lives up to Mencken's requirements of superiority to (mere) norms. To be "gorgeous" is not to wear a particular kind of suit but to manifest essences: personality and will are the qualities that are "gorgeous." As we have seen, the Fitzgeralds arrived at Oxford "gorgeously at twilight," a way of stating their own romantic readiness for experience. There is a sustained consideration of the idea at the end of Fitzgerald's essay on his own "Early Success." The extraordinary last paragraph of this meditation begins with the statement that "the compensation of a very early success is a conviction that life is a romantic matter." It ends by defining success as a compression of past and future, dream and fact, "in a single gorgeous moment."[34] But it is a Keatsian moment, not to be experienced again. A good deal more remains to be said of this point, and I will return to it.

Mencken's hero differs from the man with an entirely different set of virtues and limitations, the man who has only "the power of self-control well developed." The latter is like Nick Carraway before experience changes him. The fate of this man who is wholly conventional is to be led and inspired by "courage"—a phrase Mencken keeps repeating.[35] (In 1920, Ardita, the female lead of "The Offshore Pirate," also repeats the phrase a number of times in order to define life's most important quality.)

Fitzgerald briefly took up the idea of Nietzschean heroism, writing in 1923 about genius that "conceives a cosmos with such transcendental force that it supersedes, in certain sensitive minds, the cosmos of which they have been previously aware."[36] He is, I think, alluding to Mencken's chapter "Beyond Good and Evil," which argues the relativity of ideas, none of which are immutable, and all of which "continue in force" only until an intellectual hero chooses to displace them.[37] It must have been a pleasing and definitively romantic theme for an ambitious novelist, but it served only for temporary use. There is finally the reiterated Mencken theme of false aristocracy, which is also a Fitzgerald constant: Tom Buchanan may be adumbrated in the figure of the patrician who rules only because he is "in possession of a large share of the world's wealth." This character type is in general unfit to think; part of the comedy of his life is his continual stumbling upon (the text of *The Great Gatsby* associates the term with Tom Buchanan) varieties of false "ideas."[38]

From the appearance of his booklist to the 1926 essay "How to Waste Material," Fitzgerald mentions dozens of contemporary names and titles. He brings to bear a number of romantic ideas (nearly all of whose patterns have been charted by M. H. Abrams in his magisterial study of romantic poetry and philosophy, *Natural Supernaturalism*). One of these pieces, Fitzgerald's review of Thomas Boyd's war novel *Through the Wheat*, centers on the combination of realistic detail and romantic understanding—evidently an ideal combination: "At first the very exactitude of the detail makes one expect no more than another piece of expert reporting, but gradually the thing begins to take on significance and assume a definite and arresting artistic contour." It is the romantic credo of endowing matter with significant form. Boyd's great accomplishment is to have conveyed meaning through "sudden flashes and illuminations," a phrase with an enormous freight of literary implication and history. First, Fitzgerald states that Boyd's commonplace images have been raised to a new kind of consciousness: the sound of gunfire, the sight of yellow wheat, the sensation of being "heavy footed and blind with sweat."[39] This heightened perception corresponds to what Abrams has described as one of the most basic of romantic modes, making familiar things new through "freshness of sensation," a term he takes from Coleridge. Here is Abrams on the representation of the familiar in new tactical form: "Coleridge's passages in the *Biographia* incorporate, in precise summation, the key terms in the Romantic lexicon of creative perception. The persistent enterprise is to make the old world new not by distorting it, but by defamiliarizing the familiar through a refreshed way of looking upon it."[40] It is of course more difficult with each generation to be original, but Fitzgerald recognizes that *renewal* is an important function of description. It is good to recognize the process of allusion, but Fitzgerald constantly modifies his allusions.

It may be even more important to recognize the critical argument embodied within that descriptive phrase "sudden flashes and illuminations." This is a recalled phrase, and goes to the heart both of Fitzgerald's criticism and of *The Great Gatsby*. Abrams reminds us that suddenness and spontaneity are definitively romantic qualities. In order to express those qualities, romantics (for example, both Goethe and Wordsworth) began to use a language of "flashes" and luminescence. Particular texts seem to have been on Fitzgerald's mind: Wordworth's "flashes, as it were" of "objects recognis'd / In flashes." Abrams calls this language "revelatory and luminous," in style and intention, citing Wordsworth's "gleams / Of soul-illumination."[41] These revived terms display allegiance to a particular view, and even a particular critical vocabulary.

That "fine balance of truth in observing" that Coleridge admires in Wordsworth is rephrased, put to work when Fitzgerald praises the right use of "exactitude of detail."[42] We recall that romanticism *rejected* the overly elaborated. That is the context for Fitzgerald's conclusion: "There is a fine unity about it all. . . . The effect is cumulative . . . there are no skies and stars and dawns pointed out to give significance to the insignificant. . . . There are no treasured-up reactions to aesthetic phenomena poured along the pages . . . for sweetening purposes."[43] He is, in other words, locating his own criticism within the argument for imagination over mere fancy.

The Boyd review also contains a citation from Conrad that looks very much like garden-variety romanticism, a panegyric to youth and the past. But it is a complex allusion, referring to the first step of an imaginative process: "I remember my youth and the feeling that will never come back any more—the feeling that I could last forever, outlast the sea, the earth, and all men . . . the triumphant conviction of strength, the heat of life in the handful of dust, the glow in the heart that with every year grows dim, grows cold, grows small, and expires too soon—before life itself." Fitzgerald has a powerful literary-historical eye. He writes of this passage (it is from Conrad's *Youth*) that it is not only a remarkable block of English prose but that it has a special status for his own generation. Since reading the story, Fitzgerald has found nothing else with its weight of ideas. We recall that the movement from youth to regretful age is one of the central patterns of romantic thought, encountered most notably in *Tintern Abbey*. There are many sources, both in romantic poetry and philosophy. Common to all is a dialectical development from unconscious being to the recognition that, although "time is past," life must be re-created.[44]

Fitzgerald's invocation of Conrad corresponds to one of the major "forms" or patterns of romantic thought outlined by M. H. Abrams, who argues that the subject refers to mind's "difficulties, sufferings, and recurrent disasters in quest of a goal which, unwittingly, is the place it had left behind when it first sets out." It has little to do with nostalgia. Wordsworth had concluded that our losses lead us to participation in necessity; Keats, responding to Wordsworth's point, concluded that the pattern of loss from youth to age was in fact the central "simile of human life."[45] The view was necessarily tragic, *and to cite one part of it was to imply the rest.*

Fitzgerald's own fiction contains allusions directing the reader to romantic theory. For example, in "Winter Dreams" (1922), the story of loss and decay is not left to its own telling, as would be the case in Hemingway. At the end of Fitzgerald's story, two narrative voices discuss what has happened and what it means. It is left to its protagonist to fit events into larger patterns of meaning, i.e., to make them romantically explicit. Youth and love "had existed, and they existed no longer. . . . The gates were closed, the sun was gone down, and there was no beauty but the gray beauty of steel that withstands all time." The country of youth, Fitzgerald concludes, is "the country of illusion."[46] Even the self now is gone. It is a rephrasal of Keatsian doctrine about loss being "the simile of life." Not for the last time, Fitzgerald places the critic within the piece.

We can see this in *The Great Gatsby*, whose sixth chapter involves the reader in much more than Gatsby's own particular slice of the universal past. The romantic sense of the past is embedded in the dialogue:

"I wouldn't ask too much of her," I ventured. "You can't repeat the past."

> "Can't repeat the past?" he cried incredulously. "Why of course you can!"
>
> He looked around him wildly, as if the past were lurking here in the shadow of his house, just out of reach of his hand.
>
> "I'm going to fix everything just the way it was before," he said, nodding determinedly. "She'll see."[47]

Nick recognizes that Gatsby has never made the leap from self to actual world. Milton R. Stern puts the matter this way: Gatsby "sums up our American desire to believe in a release from history." That too has become part of our "romantic sense of self."[48]

Just after this, Nick tries to account for Gatsby's ideas, invoking "a fragment of lost words" that have been lost to memory. It is a parabolical statement: Gatsby's ideas are opaque to himself but transparent to Nick, while those fragmented words may be lost to Nick but definitely should be known to us. We are directed toward them, made to understand that somewhere in our reading minds there are phrases explaining such emotions. We may or may not find them, but they should probably be dated sometime between 1798 and 1820.[49]

Isaiah Berlin argues that one important point remains unsaid when the "form" of the simile of human life is used by poetry. Romantic entropy goes against the dream of progress, one of several dreams that romanticism is wise enough to disbelieve. Berlin's chapter on the effect of romantic ideas is much taken up with their sense of temporality, of light growing dim and heat growing cold. According to Berlin, this is more than a sensibility of self-doubt or failure: it leads to the accurate understanding of history, more accurate than that sanctioned by the institutions of education and government.[50] For Berlin, natural change (and decline) are poised against those supposedly "stable, unalterable" forces of civilized progress *that are themselves constructs if not myths*. We recall that the only man in *Gatsby* who is left with a belief in the force—and in the forces—of "civilization" is Tom Buchanan. He is a prisoner of his own mythology, arguing in vain for something that romantic knowledge defines as an impossibility: stasis understood as the status quo.

Lionel Trilling suggested that behind Fitzgerald there was indeed a great line going back to Stendhal, Byron, and Goethe, and that Fitzgerald's allusions intentionally bring to mind the ideas of Wordsworth, Keats, and Shelley.[51] Fitzgerald corroborates this when he insists on the term "romantic" as a synonym for critical thought about writing. I will review briefly his use of the term. First, it generally implies that the mode of realism is insufficient, requiring the conceptual power of romantic structure to complete its work. To describe mere detail is certainly to achieve accuracy, but only as a photograph does. As René Wellek has pointed out, the description of reality does nothing to help understand it: "Without symbol and myth the poet would lack the tools for the insight into reality which he claimed."[52] Second, writing is rarely helped by the overlay of external ideas, even of romantic ideas. Fitzgerald's 1926 essay on "How to Waste Material" rejects the wholesale application of Wells or Marx or Herbert Spencer or others to novels unconnected to them. He had enormous contempt for the practice of dressing things up to produce only "a pretty and romantic story."[53] He was not impressed by appeals to lost innocence, or the use of pastoral, or the evocation of feeling by inflating language, or by the mandatory references of contemporary fiction to "youth." Third, and most important, he revived what scholars have called the essential "forms" or patterns of romanticism: notable among them the rediscovery of experience; the cycle of development from unconscious youth to adult knowledge; the restructuring of the familiar through unremitting reform of language. This was a major intellectual accomplishment. If we think of him as the last of the romantics, that really means he is the last writer able to bring indispensable philosophical ideas to bear on his work. It might be looked at this way: the "forms" or patterns set by Wordsworth are not diminished when Fitzgerald uses them. One might even say that they have been enlarged, made relevant again.

Fitzgerald was from time to time fascinated by historical theories but remained suspicious of their promise to make life intelligible. In the writing that I have gone over we see very little that is redemptive and a great deal that is not. The essay by Trilling remains indispensable as a commentary on Fitzgerald's romantic common sense about the "social order." He was intelligently immune to the desire of his moment for ideological conformity. When he said that intelligence might consist of holding contradictory ideas simultaneously he was making a judgment of some weight. To read over Irving Babbitt or Paul Elmer More is to see that literary ideas had become confused with morals—something that seems to be happening all over again. As to the dangers of romantic thinking, Fitzgerald refused critical advice. He was smarter than the pedants who irritated his mind into creativity. As we go over his critical writings and his fiction we can see that he is rarely fooled by any kind of promise to redress nature outside of art: experience cannot be mastered, and only rarely well expressed. Perhaps that ought to be understood as his own negative capability.

❧ 2 ❧

America in Fitzgerald

In 1927, two years after *The Great Gatsby* appeared, Charles A. and Mary R. Beard published *The Rise of American Civilization*. I think that the operative words in that title need to be examined before we decide on what F. Scott Fitzgerald's idea of America may have been. In the twenties the use of the term "America" did not represent the same values or provoke the same critical reactions as it does now. It was a much less political term, which was natural enough because policy was less of an issue in national intellectual life. The great analyses of public life by Van Wyck Brooks, Walter Lippmann, H. L. Mencken, George Santayana, and Fitzgerald himself among many others are rarely about policy, but they are precisely about those terms "Rise" and "Civilization." It would have been difficult, perhaps impossible, for any idea of "America" to be separated from them, and from certain other formulations.

The subject "American civilization" brought out different levels of seriousness. The national conversation included Lippmann and Alfred North Whitehead on the meaning of the idea of progress, and also George Babbitt's pious conviction that America was booster heaven, progress in its final and absolute form—"success." What follows is the last page and peroration of the Beard history. It is considerably more factual than the last page of *The Great Gatsby* but far less convincing:

> There was no doubt about the nature of the future in America. The most common note of assurance was belief in unlimited

progress—the continuous fulfillment of the historic idea which had slowly risen through the eighteenth and nineteenth century to a position of commanding authority. Concretely it meant an invulnerable faith in democracy . . . a faith in the efficacy of that new and mysterious instrument of the modern mind, "the invention of invention," moving from one technological triumph to another . . . effecting an ever wider distribution of the blessings of civilization . . . and through the cumulative forces of intellectual and artistic reactions, conjuring from the vasty deeps of the nameless and unknown creative imagination of the noblest order, subduing physical things to the empire of the spirit—doubting not the capacity of the Power that had summoned into being all patterns of the past and present, living and dead, to fulfill its endless destiny. If so, it is the dawn, not the dusk, of the gods.[1]

This is not what Fitzgerald had in mind, even so early as his great and intuitive myth of American entropy "The Diamond as Big as the Ritz." The passage reminds us forcibly of Hemingway's opinion that fiction about history was better than history about history. Nevertheless, the concepts invoked by the Beards were in fact the subject of that "creative imagination of the noblest order." But these two writers had different opinions about progress, America, and civilization.

There is more than one meaning for many an important term.[2] The idea of civilization seems non-contentious, but the term was characteristically in dispute in the twenties. Freud stated at the end of the decade that civilization is "the whole sum of the achievements and the regulations which distinguish our lives from those of our animal ancestors and which serve two purposes—namely to protect men against nature and to adjust their mutual relations."[3] That was certainly an accurate statement, but its studied neutrality of tone does not suggest the deep divisions of the time. Although often invoked and even more often implied, the idea of "civilization" was used in different ways. Here is a brief outline:

(1) "Civilization" could be a polemical term used with happy imprecision to make judgments about American character and identity.

Magazines such as the *Saturday Evening Post* invoked it when comparing the febrile present to the vital past; this exercise was reflexive in the early twenties. It was not an innocent concept either in the *Post* or in books by Madison Grant (*The Passing of the Great Race*) and Lothrop Stoddard (*The Rising Tide of Color against White World-Supremacy*), which defined the elusive quality of Americanism, restricting it to Nordics or Anglo-Saxons. So, when Tom Buchanan says in *The Great Gatsby* that "Civilization's going to pieces," there are echoes meant to be heard. To allude to "civilization" is often to assume a nativist public role, and Tom means dimly to restore values of the American past by imposing distinctions of class, race, and religion. He is repeating the arguments of Grant, Stoddard, and also the highly popular Hendrik Willem Van Loon, who keeps those two terms "America" and "civilization" firmly connected. When Van Loon says that after the war "America has suddenly been called upon to carry forward the work of civilization," he means that we should be free of the contaminants of modernity, chief among them immigration. According to Van Loon, "The latest shipment of released Ellis Islanders" will make a new home "among the neglected residences of your own grandfathers and uncles."[4] His works, one guesses, are among Tom's "deep books with long words in them."[5]

(2) But, "the salvaging of this western civilization" could also be a project of a much different kind. An argument for assimilation of the new was made during the twenties—with great skill and much decency—by Walter Lippmann, John Dewey, and other pragmatists.[6] They opposed nativism in Dewey's essays on community, Lippmann's books on the concept of the "public," and certainly in Mencken's gadfly attacks on provincial mentality. Perhaps most important, these writers maintained a constant attack on the simplifiers. As Lippmann put the matter shortly before the twenties, "the past which men create for themselves is a place where thought is unnecessary and happiness inevitable."[7] "Civilization" was a concept and a myth often on his own mind, but it was not a given and it required constant renewal. Here is Edmund Wilson's panoramic view of the argument for change: "Think how many remarkable American books have been published in the last year—*Main Street, The Age of Innocence, The Ordeal of Mark Twain,* and Mencken's second series of *Prejudices*—and think how

they were all of them written to tell what a terrible place America is. ... It is rather tragic when you think about it, but actually I believe it is a cause for rejoicing: presumably, this devastating criticism of America is a prelude to its being made what the above authors want to see it become."[8]

The rubric of "Civilization" assimilated many things that we might think were outside its normal boundaries. It may be helpful to outline some of its principal meanings in the five-year period before *The Great Gatsby*. In 1920, George Santayana's *Character and Opinion in the United States* began by referring to the perilous condition of "Civilisation" in the United States. For Santayana, character and mind were connected to the past. He was more sympathetic to change than one might think, but he believed that the American problem was its need to check "liberty" by self-discipline. His definition of "civilised life" was a life within limits, guided by the lessons of the past. From this it was a short jump to his conception of a new, idealistic, but essentially unbalanced American character that might never recognize the boundaries of reality.[9] H. L. Mencken contributed his own philosophical pessimism, writing in 1921 about the *decline* of American "civilization," which was most visible below the Mason-Dixon Line. For years, Mencken had turned out essays that skewered the provincialism of the South, its religion, letters, politics, and style. But more was involved than satire: the South lived in the unusable past, "sentimentalizing the civilization that had collapsed and departed."[10] His South is in many respects the model for Fitzgerald's own fallen "civilization" of Tarleton, Georgia, a cultural empty space encouraging early departure. Mencken's "The Sahara of the Bozart" was a scorched-earth comparison of provincial America with provincial Europe, infinitely to our disadvantage. It had great resonance, and when reprinted in *Prejudices: Second Series* was reviewed by Fitzgerald.[11] In 1922, Harold E. Stearns published *Civilization in the United States,* a study of virtually all the defects of American national character as perceived by intellectuals. This anthology contains an important essay on the literary life by Van Wyck Brooks, who made the reiterated point that "civilization" even in "the Eastern states" may be "running to seed." For Brooks, "our civilization" is simply a synonym for "the waste and futility of American life" as displayed by Theodore Dreiser and experienced by all writers.[12] The view was widely shared, and is more convincing than claims for the influence of Spengler.[13] (For example, Edmund Wilson observed "how much Thoreau's assault on American civilization sounds like that of Van Wyck Brooks or of some other young intellectual of today."[14]) Other works by Brooks, such as *America's Coming-of-Age,* examine at length the decline of national powers and individual character under the rubric of "Civilization."[15] In 1923, Grant Overton's *American Night's Entertainment* appeared, referring the argument over change in our national character to Shaw, Wells, George Horace Lorimer, Madison Grant, Lothrop Stoddard, and others who thought rightly, including Warren G. Harding. Overton writes about race and immigration as subjects that might well have inflamed the Tom Buchanan type—any reader of Lothrop Stoddard (who is thinly disguised in *The Great Gatsby* as "this man Goddard") being "bound to be carried to a high pitch of enthusiastic affirmation or else roused to fierce resentment and furious denial."[16] In 1924, Irving Babbitt tried to make some sense of the issue, but the idea of American "civilization" had become bound up in debates over race and immigration.[17] In 1925, at a level much higher than the participants in national debate were likely to understand, Alfred North Whitehead wrote some pregnant essays on the radical inconsistency "in our civilization" (i.e., our faith divided between mechanism and will), which left a mark on at least one reviewer, Edmund Wilson.[18]

(3) A third way of thought introduced some disturbing new variables. I think that the best place to start with this category is in 1930 with Freud's famous question at the beginning of *Civilization and Its Discontents*: "How has it happened," he asked, "that so many people have come to take up this strange attitude of hostility to civilization?"[19] It is a postwar question, but with prewar components. At the end of the nineteenth century, some versions of his question were stated in works of fiction. Victorian escapism, especially the works of Sir Arthur Conan Doyle, H. Rider Haggard, and H. G. Wells, was especially rich in the depiction of civilized inauthenticity. *The Time Machine* rejects the idea of progress, which becomes replaced by a kind of massive, unconscious entropy—even by regress. And in *Allan Quatermain* we see the Freudian premise already shaped: the "heart rises up in rebellion

against the strict limits of the civilised life.... When the heart is stricken, and the head is humbled in the dust, civilisation fails us utterly."[20] It was an idea awaiting a cause, and that came with the Great War. There was extensive disillusion with "an old bitch gone in the teeth ... a botched civilization."[21]

This is a theme of postwar writing central to the criticism of Pound and Eliot.[22] But the theme showed itself in more than literary criticism. Here is part of a conversation on a bus going from Coney Island to Delancey Street: "'By the way . . . where did you get that line about "the downfall of western civilization"?—You know, that night I took you to the movies, you said that you probably looked like the downfall of western civilization.' 'Oh,' she said, 'that was just something I picked up at the Ritz Bar in Paris'!"[23] The passage, which is from Edmund Wilson's *I Thought of Daisy* (1929), suggests why the theme is so rich in ironies, and also why it should be present in Fitzgerald, Hemingway, and others who were suspicious about the idea of progress. One of the great passages in the debate on Western civilization was written in 1930 by Ludwig Wittgenstein:

> I realize then that the disappearance of a culture does not signify the disappearance of human value, but simply of certain means of expressing this value, yet the fact remains that I have no sympathy for the current of European civilization and do not understand its goals, if it has any. . . . It is all one to me whether the typical western scientist understands or appreciates my work, since he will not in any case understand the spirit in which I write. Our civilization is characterized by the word "progress." Progress is its form rather than making progress being one of its features. Typically it constructs. It is occupied with building an ever more complicated structure. And even clarity is sought only as a means to this end, not as an end in itself. For me on the contrary clarity, perspicuity are valuable in themselves.[24]

The argument over decline and fall was conducted at some distance over Tom Buchanan's head and he hears mainly echoes of its theories.

This particular passage supports Spengler, and implicitly attacks scientific optimism in the late twenties. The passage is indispensable for anyone working on the idea of metaphysical or even social "clarity" in *A Farewell to Arms*.

Such arguments will surface in Fitzgerald's life and works, as in a column from *The New York World* of 3 April 1927 which breathlessly claims that "F. Scott Fitzgerald is a Nietzschean, F. Scott Fitzgerald is a Spenglerian, F. Scott Fitzgerald is in a state of cosmic despair."[25] It is not a serious piece, but the interviewer understands that the idea of cultural entropy is now recognizably within the jigsaw puzzle of American consciousness. I have noted in the preceding chapter Fitzgerald's statement of 1921 about race and the cycles of history. He notes therein that he and Zelda "carefully reconstructed an old theory" of decline and fall.[26] Fitzgerald continued working with the idea in *The Beautiful and Damned* (1922), a novel that is organized around what might well be called the idea of regress. He kept returning to the subject in his many stories—in their way Faulknerian—about the American South.

Ideas of "civilization" played against one another. In the Introduction to *Civilization in the United States*, Stearns picks up the main tendencies and reminds his readers of an argument over a generation old:

> Whatever else American civilization is, it is not Anglo-Saxon . . . we shall never achieve any genuine nationalistic self-consciousness as long as we allow certain financial and social minorities to persuade us that we are still an English colony. Until we begin seriously to appraise and warmly to cherish the heterogeneous elements which make up our life, and to see the common element running through all of them, we shall make not even a step towards true unity; we shall remain, in Roosevelt's class-conscious and bitter but illuminating phrase, a polyglot boardinghouse.[27]

Part of the "civilization" debate, this was also part of a dialogue of generations. Stearns spent a great deal of time identifying the men and ideas important to his education, and George Santayana had been chief among them. He was the greatest teacher at Harvard, at least as Stearns saw things, even when matched against Josiah Royce, Irving Babbitt, and George Lyman Kittredge.[28] But, the ideas that Santayana propagated about civilization in 1905 were no longer acceptable in 1922. In order to understand the student we have to understand the teacher. Here is the other half of the dialectic:

> Blood is the ground of character and intelligence. The fruits of civilisation may, indeed, be transmitted from one race to another and consequently a certain artificial homogeneity may be secured amongst different nations; yet unless continual intermarriage takes place each race will soon recast and vitiate the common inheritance. . . . Community of race is a far deeper bond than community of language, education, or government.[29]

Fitzgerald took the argument over American civilization and gave it a local habitation and a name. That is not to say he can automatically be understood by using twenty-first-century standards. At various times Fitzgerald described America as an idea rather than a land or a people ("The Swimmers"); as a republic, a set of institutions, and a race ("Six of One—"); as a site yet uncivilized ("Rags Martin-Jones and The pr-nce of w-les"); as a marketplace ("May Day"); as the scene of progress and expansion and also of failure ("The Diamond as Big as the Ritz"); as a battlefield of northern money and southern history ("The Ice Palace"); and as a new set of experiences set uneasily upon the cultural landmarks of mid-Victorianism ("Dice, Brassknuckles & Guitar").[30] In *The Great Gatsby* it is a foregone dream.

American history is an ambiguous subject in Fitzgerald. What might be called the undesired history of the North is conveniently forgotten in "The Ice Palace," while the history of the West is manufactured with government connivance in "The Diamond as Big as the Ritz." The history of the South so important to Sally Carroll Happer is "scarcely remembered" in "The Jelly-Bean" (143). The history of the East is the end both of *The Great Gatsby* and also of the Puritan interpretation of the settlement of the New World. Common to these texts are the themes of rise and also *decline*.

The Great Gatsby takes us back to the colonies and before, but Fitzgerald's focus on American history is the period after the Civil War. The historical past to which he often refers is composed of the Gilded Age, Imperial America, and the Machine Age. However, he does not draw the pious lesson from them of any "rise" in American "civilization."[31] He uses the term "Victorian" a good deal, with some nostalgia, insisting on the importance of the broken connection between then and now. As for specific chronology, Fitzgerald repeatedly describes the three-generation sequence from about 1860 to about 1920. For example, "The Ice Palace" (1920) knows that "there was something" before our time. One of its great scenes is the American past itself in a country churchyard: "They passed through the gateway and followed a path that led through a wavy valley of graves—dusty-gray and mouldy for the fifties; quaintly carved with flowers and jars for the seventies; ornate and hideous for the nineties, with fat marble cherubs lying in sodden sleep on stone pillows, and great impossible growths of nameless granite flowers. Occasionally they saw a kneeling figure with tributary flowers, but over most of the graves lay silence and withered leaves with only the fragrance that their own shadowy memories could waken in living minds" (52). Fitzgerald's work will interrupt, even derail, straight-line narrative: "The Diamond as Big as the Ritz" hesitates in the village of Fish, *The Great Gatsby* stops in the Valley of Ashes, and this story too refuses to proceed into the present. All three narratives are informed by the American cathexis, an overpowering investment of psychic energy in action. But when we come to those rows of Confederate dead, the idea of America becomes more complex. It is not a matter entirely of energies but of time-bound meanings. They are difficult to state both for Sally Carroll and for F. Scott Fitzgerald, appearing as not-quite-defined "dreams" of a better self and a better age. We are, I think, expected to understand their Platonic implications, especially the values of stasis.

The spirit of lost place and time confronts that of the mechanic North, with its expensive things "that all looked about fifteen years old." Here is the history of the North understood only through characteristically American subjectivity: "This is a three-generation town. Everybody has a father, and about half of us have grandfathers. Back of that we don't go" (56). Fitzgerald understands that the North—which has become America—has no history past memory. When in "Babylon Revisited" we read that "the present was the thing" (628), that is only another way of stating this idea of America. There are few other values, which is why Lorraine in that story intuitively claims that "everybody seems so old lately, but I don't feel old a bit" (629). Perhaps Myrtle Wilson puts the issue most forcibly in *The Great Gatsby* when she says that "You can't live forever, you can't live forever." Essentially without a past, living only to escape it, she knows also that life doesn't go any distance into the future either. The idea about the absolute present in the American mind was often and ruefully noted by William James and George Santayana, with the former arguing that "the lustre of the present hour" is an intellectual illusion. The present needs to attain significance through connection to both past and future.[32] Walter Lippmann was concerned—obsessed really—with the conflict of historical, scientific, and personal conceptions of time, and made that conflict a main point of *Public Opinion* in 1922. He reviewed James's position, and added that the conception of "social time"—i.e., that not directly involving the self—was essential to democracy. That concept, linked with "duration" far beyond the moment, was common to the philosophy of both Lippmann and James.[33] Sally Carroll Happer is an important part of a dialogue beyond fiction. She too argues for what Lippmann called the "ideational present," in which "years of the past are brought together into the present." Either she knows much more than we suspect, or Fitzgerald does.

Fitzgerald's southern characters have been shaped by time and place. They are involved in a bitter dilemma: whether to live the life of progress, or to take refuge in the past. The choice is often involuntary: Jim Powell, the Jelly-bean, realizes that he has to "make somethin'" (157) out of his farm and his life, while Sally Carroll says that she needs "to live where things happen" (51). Her energies "may be useful somewhere else" (51). Energy needs a field of action, which in Fitzgerald is almost always the North or East. But energy is not mind, and has its limits. The South is, I think, substantially more than "a warm, pleasant, and lazy place, a home of good manners and elegant traditions, a garden which, for Fitzgerald, grew Southern belles and jelly-beans."[34] It may be as important a place as the garden of Andrew Marvell, offering a perspective of the unconsidered life of action—and of progress. When Fitzgerald begins a southern story by telling us that "the sunlight dripped over the houses like golden paint over an art jar" (48) he quite literally suggests the stasis of history as that of art. He characteristically uses the imagery of gold and sunlight to describe the South.

Cleanth Brooks has thought about an opposition central to our thought, and it applies to the work of Fitzgerald: "If there is a myth of the American future—its more respectable name is the American Dream—and with reference to the charge that the Southern myth erred in describing its past as golden, one might point out that the American myth has consistently insisted that its future was made of the same precious metal. But a golden future, never quite here, always about to be, may turn out to be quite as much a falsification."[35]

In 1927, Charles and Mary Beard (who may well have been reading Fitzgerald) cited the transmutation of our national wealth from "metalled mountains of Montana" to "chateaux of French design." Like Fitzgerald, they wrote that the new order was built on the ruins of slave power and had to re-create an aristocracy. But, since it was formless and without taste it violated every conceivable canon of style. This non-civilization simply amassed "statuary, paintings, pottery, rugs, and every other form of art."[36] Or, as Fitzgerald noted, "jewels, fabrics, wines, and metals" all blurred into a sweet mist of desire (190). The aboriginal Civil War generation had endowed modern America with great energies and desires, yet these mere *things* described above fail completely to correspond to the metaphysical and moral weight of those energies and desires. It is the problem of Jay Gatsby in a more general form. The arrival of the future had settled very little.

In 1937, Fitzgerald recalled his own historical sense of American life at the beginning of the twenties: "With the end of the winter set in another pleasant pumped-dry period, and while I took a little time off, a fresh picture of life in America began to form before my eyes. The uncertainties of 1919 were over—there seemed little doubt about what was going to happen—America was going on the greatest, gaudiest spree in history and there was going to be plenty to tell about it. The whole golden boom was in the air—its splendid generosities, its outrageous corruptions and the tortuous death struggle of the old America in prohibition. . . . For my point of vantage was the dividing line between the two generations."[37] We make much of the boom as a subject of his fiction, but tend to elide the story of that "dividing line" in American generational life. However, Edith Wharton (alluding to Walter Lippmann's theory of "the gulf between those days and these") found such an idea to be of consummate importance.[38] Fitzgerald's major work of 1922, *The Beautiful and Damned,* uses a generational sequence to satirize something a good deal larger and more interesting than the follies of great wealth. It gains momentum because it sticks to the great subjects of the "Civilization" debate, the loyalty of Americans to the idea of progress and the manifestation of those energies that Fitzgerald so much admired in life.

This novel's language describes the downward trajectory from great moral energies of the past to inertia and unconsciousness in the present. Its heavy investment in national psychology has certain sources. H. L. Mencken's dissenting voice had stated in 1920 that the inner life of mass man was based on "fear of the unknown, the complex, the inexplicable. What he wants beyond everything else is security. His instincts incline him toward a society so organized that it will protect him at all hazards, and not only against perils to his hide but also against assaults upon his mind—against the need to grapple with unaccustomed problems, to weigh ideas, to think things out for himself."[39] This provides a backdrop for a drama of American characters. As in other cultural-historical essays by Mencken, it hit one of the nerves of the "Civilization" argument: the open question was whether the theory of progress was based only upon the *illusion* of individual will, act, and initiative. Fitzgerald's own opinion was strongly implied in 1922 when he began working with these ideas in *The Beautiful and Damned.*

First, the manic acquisition of unsanctified wealth: "Now Adam J. Patch, more familiarly known as 'Cross Patch,' left his father's farm in Tarrytown early in sixty-one to join a New York cavalry regiment. He came home from the war a major, charged into Wall Street, and amid much fuss, fume, applause, and ill will he gathered to himself some seventy-five million dollars."[40] From which point we allegorically decline. It is plain enough that Mr. Patch has his "energies" but they quickly decline into Comstockery (the moralistic movement that is one of the great standing jokes in Mencken), and to what Fitzgerald describes as rabid monomania. Progress becomes entropy: he marries an "anaemic lady of thirty, Alicia Withers," and their son becomes known as the first man in America to roll the lapels of his coat (6). Not a William-Jamesian accomplishment. Our Anthony, in the third generation, is often tired and generally horizontal—conditions that in fiction have implications about political and social energies.

Before Daisy Buchanan wonders what people "do" with their lives, Anthony Patch has been invited "to *do* something" with his. A national issue is involved—for example, the "value as a social creature" of Gloria's father turns out to be "a black and imponderable negative" (40). In the following passage about Anthony Patch in his later life, Fitzgerald describes considerably more than an existential moment: "With a tired movement he arose and obeyed; the gray window-panes vanished. He stretched himself. He was heavier now, his stomach was a limp weight against his belt; the flesh had softened and expanded. He was thirty-two and his mind was a bleak and disordered wreck" (406). The passage uses the idiom of inversion: youth is old age, progress becomes regress. In fact, an idea about American identity is compromised. This passage should be set against Fitzgerald's Jazz Age essay on symbolic chronology: "Every day in every way [we] grew better and better . . . and it seemed only a question of a few years before the older people would step aside and let the world be run by those who saw things as they were."[41] That may have been the ideal, but it turned out not to be the standard. In *The Beautiful and Damned* the disordered body and mind are persistently connected to national character. I think that they compose the body politic, a correspondence long familiar in philosophy, revived by social thought of the twenties.

At one point, Fitzgerald uses the phrase "thoroughly un-American" (7) to describe Anthony Patch's languid, subjective personality. The phrasing is repeated: later in the narrative Gloria Gilbert wonders aloud whether inertia should be at all "possible for an American" while Anthony intentionally confuses his weakness with a more elegant European style. But his inertial passivity is more than a style. We might think of William James's analysis of 1906: "The human individual . . . possesses powers of various sorts which he habitually fails to use. He energizes below his maximum, and he behaves below his optimum. . . . Every man of woman born knows what is meant by such phrases as having a good vital tone, a high tide of spirits, an elastic temper, as living energetically, working easily, deciding firmly, and the like."[42] In Jamesian terms, these qualities make possible the good American life: the exertion of will produces conscious, meaningful acts. In James's world, no one exists alone, everyone exists in relationship to someone else. *Both individuals and nations* may be described by the same vocabulary, adding up to a vision of that oft-cited quality of American "vitality."

Anthony Patch exhibits that famous "dilemma of passivity" that James described in an essay whose title ("Is Life Worth Living?") needs to be remembered. Its point was taken up in the novel. Muriel Kane and Anthony both understand that life is a "moral multiverse" in which vitality is not only life itself but the sign of moral awareness.[43] In Jamesian terms, vitality opposes the determinism of fate—or of politics. It may then be a mistake to think of Fitzgerald's second novel as being strictly about the personal problems of youth. As James wrote in 1907, invoking the correspondence of body and mind, "democracy as a whole may undergo self-poisoning."[44] If there is the slightest doubt about this interpretation, James's editor and disciple Horace M. Kallen wrote in 1930, "Happy America! The economy of our body politic is so like the life-system of a physiological individual that the process by which a poison stimulates its own anti-bodies into existence is repeated in another form by the woes and ways of our society."[45]

Is there some specific brief in the text for this interpretation? Just after this passage, the critical Muriel Kane argues with Anthony about his passivity or entropy, saying to Gloria, "I've been talking philosophy with your husband." Anthony responds that "We took up some fundamental concepts." Again there is the connection—it seems to be natural—between body and idea. What are those "concepts" involved, what is the "philosophy," and when did both appear? I have suggested the pervasive influence of William James; and before the twenties there was Walter Lippmann's powerful tract for the times, *Drift and Mastery;*

while during the decade there were John Dewey's extraordinary essays on American character and its social condition. Lippmann describes a passive, withdrawn American figure deriving from James, one whom we will learn to recognize in Edith Wharton, in Sinclair Lewis, and in a number of F. Scott Fitzgerald texts including *The Crack-Up*. Lippmann ties the knot for us, showing just how *national* personality declines:

> Everyone has met the man who approached life eagerly and tapered off to a middle age where the effort is over. . . . Effort wells up, beats bravely against reality, and in weariness simmers down into routine or fantasy. No doubt much of this is due to physiological causes. . . . And yet in large measure the explanation lies elsewhere. . . . This abandonment of effort is due, I imagine to the fact that the conscious mastery of experience is, comparatively speaking, a new turn in human culture. . . . The modern world . . . has thrown men upon their own responsibility. And for that gigantic task they lack experience, they are fettered and bound and finally broken. . . . The sheer struggle for freedom is an exhausting thing, so exhausting that the people who lead it are often unable to appreciate its uses.[46]

In terms of representation, the subject silently changes from the individual "man" mentioned in the opening sentence to the American "people" of the last, which is to say that there has been no change of identity at all. Lippmann's theory, derived from James, understands the nation to be the individual writ large. It is important to understand the distinction that Lippmann draws between "physiological causes" and explanation that "lies elsewhere." He invites the reader to make a more than historical judgment, to think, as a novel makes us think, about the connection between body and idea. We extrapolate the meaning of that enervated American self, see it in terms not only of politics but of an issue even larger. As Lippmann puts it, we may never "attain" that elusive quality of "civilization." That is to say, we will probably fail to fulfill the idea of progress that motivated Victorianism, and that was translated into modern confidence and conscience.

At the end of the decade, John Dewey invoked the correspondence between individual and national pathology. The unrest of American life, he wrote, is "evidence, psychologically, of abnormality.... Only an acute maladjustment between individuals and the social conditions under which they live can account for such widespread pathological phenomena." He identified "nervous discontentment" and the many anxieties of private life as the signs of a new social dispensation. When we see certain patterns of "thought, imagination and emotion," Dewey adds, we must recognize that they are largely reflected "externals," which is as plain as any philosophy of correspondences is liable to get. And he too argues that the new social order may never attain that elusive quality of civilization that was so widely sought.[47] He anticipates Fitzgerald's own analysis, gives it a philosophical language. We live, Dewey writes, at a time when individuals are caught "between a past that is intellectually too empty . . . and a present that is too diversely crowded and chaotic to afford balance or direction to ideas and emotion."[48] In short, there really has been a "dividing line" between generations.

For a writer to cite the metonym of rise, decline, and fall—to embody the process in character and mentality as in Anthony Patch or Newland Archer or even in the Jelly-bean, Jim Powell—was to participate in a national argument. The terminology of health and disease, energy and attrition, vitality and passivity, is full of public implication. Fitzgerald has taken the subtext of the early twentieth century, its obsession with energy, action, progress, and becoming, and replaced it with displays of anemia, passivity, blank and unreflective suspension, unconsciousness, negation, and even delusion. His insight into the authority of failure may be a historical stance.

The "Civilization" debate is nowhere more central in Fitzgerald than at the scene in the Plaza Hotel toward the end of *The Great Gatsby* in which more than one idea becomes clarified. Tom Buchanan delivers a chaotic speech about "family life and family institutions." Nick listens to him, and suddenly understands that he is witnessing a kind of civic fantasy. It is a great comic moment, with this poseur seeing himself "standing alone on the last barrier of civilization." The moment is amplified by the reference to the pomposity and inbuilt fakery of academic art—Tom has already told us much about his sense of "art" and Nick divines the mural that is on his mind. We see Tom's assumption of fake *gravitas,* the toga spread over his vices. But, the main point is that the idea of civilization has become as unserious as the man believing in it. So, when we listen to his "impassioned gibberish" we see two kinds of farce, and one of them is about the end of a long, untenable dream about civilization in America.[49] It is nicely done, with language having the same relationship to human ascent as gibberish does to fall.

3

Edmund Wilson and Alfred North Whitehead

Like Fitzgerald, Edmund Wilson made romanticism an armature for his critical ideas in the twenties. He was absorbed by its philosophy, especially as Alfred North Whitehead was then restating it. We tend now to elide his interest. One consequence is that coverage of Edmund Wilson "in his time" gives the same kind of importance to small intellectual issues like war and taxes as to large intellectual issues such as the way he thought about books.[1]

Wilson's criticism during the twenties was to an extent derivative. He often acknowledged his debt to the philosophy of Whitehead, which had opened up an entirely new discipline beyond the abilities of literary criticism. Whitehead's was a rewarding, difficult philosophy that became central to the understanding of modernist literature.[2] Yet, if anything, Edmund Wilson's critical discoveries of the twenties seem to count for less now than they did then. Here is the deflationary account of his work by René Wellek in 1977:

> Still, there are definite limits to the reach of his mind. I am not thinking only of his obvious lack of technical skill in analyzing narrative modes or poetic structures. More disturbing is the coarseness and even vulgarity of his dominant interest in sex, displayed in some of the fiction and, obsessively, in the early notebooks. He shows hardly any interest in the fine arts or music. He lacks understanding not only for religion, which he treats as a "delusion," but for philosophy. The early enthusiasm

for Whitehead, his "crystalline abstract thought," seems to be based on a misunderstanding. It supported Wilson in his limited sympathies for symbolism and made him discount the "two divisions of mind and matter, body and soul," also in his polemics against the Neohumanists. But Wilson could not share Whitehead's neoplatonic idealism or his concept of God, and Wilson soon abandoned Whitehead for Marxism. But, as Wilson's Marxism discarded the dialectic, it meant rather a return to a basic positivism and pragmatism, a commonsense attitude to reality.[3]

This is a long indictment. I plan here not to deal at all with sex, only tangentially with religion and Marxism, and largely with Alfred North Whitehead's symbolic view of nature.

Wilson kept on restating the point that literary criticism in the twenties had no intellectual basis. The best critic, Paul Elmer More, was hopelessly retrograde—realist, classicist, moralist. But he was a worthy antagonist, and did at least know books and ideas; the rest, from Mencken to Van Wyck Brooks, were sympathetic but useless. They were without a significant theoretical language. Mencken could not discuss T. S. Eliot, and Eliot did not bother discussing Mencken. There was no "serious literary criticism."[4] Wilson came up with a recurrent answer, put here in one of its later forms: "For me, all the constructions of intellect and imagination, from poetry, drama, and fiction through Whitehead (metaphysics is the poetry and fiction of people who do not produce concrete images) to Einstein, are inventions directed to enabling us to get through life and explain the world."[5] We are familiar enough with the important last phrases about life and the world, but I think they are not fully intelligible without reference to those constructions of intellect.

Shortly after the publication of *Science and the Modern World,* Wilson began to write about and incorporate aspects of Whitehead's philosophy. His interest was lifelong but crested in the period 1925–1931. We begin with an essay in 1925 on "A. N. Whitehead and Bertrand Russell."[6] Wilson asserts that both are important, but that Whitehead is particularly a guide to the connection of science, philosophy, and literature. He was to allude to Dewey, James, Russell, Santayana, and other figures of the twenties, but Whitehead remained for him a figure of special importance. Wilson's *New Republic* review of Whitehead in 1925 makes two essential points. The first is that unlike Bertrand Russell, with whom he is being compared, Whitehead can translate from scientific into literary language "the complication by relativity of the old ideas of space and time." Because of that, Whitehead bears necessarily on the poetry of modernism, having in fact "some remarkable points of resemblance . . . to M. Paul Valéry." Wilson concluded—it may now seem an exaggeration—that Valéry and Whitehead were "among the first modern writers" to challenge scientific materialism, therefore to reassert fundamental principles of "general intellectual life."[7] There is bound to be some perplexity, but that is not because the point is unimportant; it is only that, having ourselves crossed the divide, we do not have the perspective to tell the difference between the natural and its current interpretation.

Wilson and Whitehead rejected the confident application of scientific analogy to thought. Here is a sardonic, worst-case example from *I Thought of Daisy*: "Were not imagination and reason like the phagocytes of our physical nature, which, as soon as an infection occurs, rush to mass themselves at the breach, where they ingest the disturbing intruders and put a stop to the progress of the disease?"[8] Analogy is tempting, but Whitehead scholarship reminds us not to assume that commonplace observation based on "clear and distinct sensory experiences" can be applied in ordinary life. Such transference was a constant irritant to Whitehead, who provided a vision of life as it might conventionally be seen by materialism: "A bit of matter is . . . a passive fact, an individual reality which is the same at an instant, or throughout a second, an hour, or a year. . . . Each bit of matter occupies a definite limited region. Each such particle . . . has its own private qualification; such as its shape, its motion, its mass. . . . Some of these qualifications change, others are persistent. The essential relationship between bits of matter is purely spatial. Space itself is eternally unchanging, always including in itself this capacity for the relationship of bits of matter."[9] One substitutes the term "human" for the term "matter." There is perhaps no more important influence on Wilson than Whitehead's idea that the varieties of experience cannot be understood through any single scientific model, nor a more important argument (it is also Whitehead's) that Shelley was a better judge of phenomena than Leibniz. In *Axel's Castle,* Wilson was eventually to write that we cannot "put our finger on the point where the novelist or poet stops and the scientist or metaphysician begins."[10]

Modernism became associated with hostility to romanticism, but Wilson valued Whitehead because of his sympathy for it.[11] The issue seems distant but is connected to Wilson's theory of literature, and also to his politics. One of Wilson's first moves was to revalue romantic poetry, which he now understood to be a reaction to (and remedy for scientific) generalization. After stating the great accomplishments of Blake and Wordsworth, Wilson invoked new authority to explain their importance: "As Whitehead says, they had ceased to describe the world as a machine, but recreated it as an organism."[12] In the twenties that was familiar enough ground, but Wilson thought there were a number of revaluations yet to be made. He argued that the modern biological sciences—the idea of evolution itself—had contributed to the mechanistic interpretation of our minds and actions. And Wilson located the most devastating literary effects of mechanism in the line of philosophical poetry from Pope through Tennyson, a way of thinking and writing that was brilliantly explicit but completely without emotional impact. There were a good many French connections, particularly in the work of those "naturalistic" writers whose aim was to produce descriptions that were "solid, economical, and exact."[13] This particular issue was to be on Wilson's mind for the next two years, culminating in his plan for *Axel's Castle.*[14] However, at this point, in 1926, Wilson was preoccupied with the problem of the "exact objective reproduction" of "subjective phenomena," a problem that the romantics knew had yet to be solved.[15]

Phenomena were, Wilson realized, too various to be understood through scientific objectivity. While romanticism had been our principal mode of recognizing that, it was no longer tenable. Yet, its work might be reinforced: "The real counterpart of the first romantic movement" might be, he wrote, "the French 'symbolism' of the end of the century."

He has this to say about the connection: "The function of symbolism was to make things unscientific . . . to transfer the scene of the artist's operations from the external to the internal world." In brief, modernism "has its roots in symbolism," while symbolism has its roots in romantic metaphysics.[16] Wilson's second piece on Whitehead ends by poising Shelley and Wordsworth against scientific explanation of phenomena.

The third and longest piece on Whitehead appeared in the *New Republic* in 1927. Beginning with an extensive account of Whitehead's career, the essay homes in on the work from 1919 to 1926, i.e., the period in which *Science and the Modern World* and *Religion in the Making* appeared. It is especially concerned with the concept and *mode* of symbolic logic, a subject to which I will return. Wilson's essay is at times simply a vehicle for Norman Kemp Smith's introduction to Whitehead on nature, a pamphlet cited in great detail over a number of pages. Smith was drawn to the Whitehead ideas I have cited, arguing, for example, that when physics conceives of "bits of matter . . . moving in space" it confuses the issue of material and other, equally natural entities.[17] The material, according to Smith's understanding of Whitehead (and clearly also to Wilson's), has no definitive connection to the mental. If only to understand Wilson on experience, we need to absorb Smith's assessment of Whitehead on nature:

> The living organism "must be interpreted in the same general manner as atoms and molecules. . . . Life is too obstinately concrete" to be located in an instant, even if at the instant it be spread over a space. Thus nature, as envisaged by Whitehead, is extraordinarily different from nature as defined in terms of classical physics. While less tidy, with all sorts of loose ends, it is allowed to have more content; and in proportion as it has become more bewildering, just thereby it has become more and more like unto the reality which faces us in experience. In view of the amazing diversity of the items which, on Whitehead's view, compose nature—the tastes as well as the textures of foods, the roar of the lion and the song of the nightingale as well as the labyrinthine structures of the inner ear, the gorgeous

coloration of the peacock's tail as well as the rods and cones of the retina—nature, thus envisaged, will at every turn, to the great benefit of our open-mindedness, force upon our attention the immense gaps, not merely in our detailed and established theories, but also even in our most conjectural interpretations of nature's doings.[18]

Here are the points that Wilson himself raises after repeated citation of Norman Kemp Smith: (1) Whitehead is skeptical of Einstein's thesis about the nature of space and time. I doubt that Wilson was capable of adjudicating the dispute, but he did have an important reason for referring to it. The Whitehead view restores some kind of predictability, "making the universe seem somewhat less fantastic than, on Einstein's view, it must appear."[19] This needs to be looked at in terms of its social implications because we recall Wellek's observation that for Wilson, after Whitehead came Marx. (2) After reference to Whitehead's *Science in the Modern World* and *Religion in the Making,* and also to a series of reviews of these works in the *New Republic* by Dewey, Russell, and others, Wilson states his indifference to the argument between science and theology. What matters to him is intellectual plenitude, the number of ways to reach truth. (3) He then makes the point that readers are indebted to Whitehead for applying "modern physical theory" to "other departments of thought, to bring it forward into metaphysics, into literature and into theology."[20] Whitehead is identified, in fact, as himself a modernist, familiar with the literature of modernism, able to unify "a variety of fields of experience." He is one of three figures—the others being Proust and Valéry—with this capacity. (4) Whitehead's modernism and his importance to intellectuals is nowhere more emphatic than in his symbolic reasoning. (5) Finally, the claim is made that Whitehead provides "necessary significance to a world of which the old accepted meanings have so disastrously come to be discredited."[21] There is no point to going over Whitehead on relativity, and Wilson himself gratefully gave up any consideration of his mathematics, but we can learn a good deal from Whitehead's ideas—not all mentioned above—in Wilson's text. For one thing, Wilson's novel of the late twenties, *I Thought of Daisy,* not only introduces those ideas (they are discussed by narrator and protagonists) but absorbs Whitehead's language into his own.

So far as Wilson was concerned, Whitehead's two central works were *Science in the Modern World* and the essays on symbolic logic.[22] He drew from the former a history and a theory, and from the latter a method. I have cited Wilson's *New Republic* essay that surveys ideas from Pope to Tennyson, ideas that seem to come from literary history. But they came from Whitehead's fifth chapter of *Science and the Modern World.* Both poets are treated by Whitehead as casualties in the intellectual wars of science: the first a too-confident defender of mechanism, the second an opponent of "general mechanical laws" reducing all life to the same scale. In that chapter ("The Romantic Reaction") Whitehead makes the point that Wordsworth is our greatest literary-philosophical figure because of his mastery of "the concrete facts of our apprehension." Shelley is almost as important because his "nature is a nature of organisms" and his language the most successful at stating perceptual experience.[23]

So far as Whitehead is concerned, romantic poetry is scientific testimony. It remains the best way of getting at "objects of sense" and understanding recurrent experience. These ideas are written into *Axel's Castle.*[24] One conclusion of Whitehead's is especially important because it names what he considers to be the work of literary statement: "We gain from the poets the doctrine that a philosophy of nature must concern itself at least with these six notions: change, value, eternal objects, endurance, organism, interfusion." Poetry is always "evidence" of these characteristics to Whitehead, an idea that did not escape Wilson. And writing is the great mode of approaching if not solving the great problem of "obstinate, irreducible, limited facts." To the degree possible, writing explains the world through observing phenomena.[25] Many of these ideas were quickly put to work by Wilson in his own criticism and fiction.

I Thought of Daisy records the narrator's search for love, literature, and meaning in life—quantities with only marginal value in our marketplace culture. Wilson's narrator moves among disarmed intellectuals whose lives are chaotic and ineffective, as are their explanations for those lives. One of these intellectuals, Hugo Bamman, a writer who takes ideas seriously, cannot do the same with people. He has been allegorically wounded, unable to connect the three great matters of art, love, and meaning. His life is characterized by habitual distancing from things human. People are embodied ideas. As the novel puts it, he drank in company, and listened, then pickled a specimen for his notebooks. Deeply conscious of money and class, Bamman had come to distrust his own family, who were, he thought, mindless capitalists. But, although he chose to live among bohemians and radicals he never trusted their judgment and could not be one of them. He remained as an observer, representing artistic "detachment" and something more.

Alfred North Whitehead appears as a leading character, Professor Grosbeake. (This character is also partly based on Christian Gauss, Wilson's mentor at Princeton.)[26] He exists in *I Thought of Daisy* not entirely because scientific materialism needs to be confronted with romantic epistemology—although that happens. He is there because what is material needs to be redefined. In this novel, Whitehead-Gauss-Grosbeake is as important an existential figure as he is a philosopher. The novel is concerned principally with experience, his understanding of it, and his effect on the mind of the narrator. His presence is important, because it allows the appearance in fiction of ideas from Whitehead's works.

Grosbeake is not alone in the effect he makes: at one point the narrator stops, and reflects that "the entrance of Grosbeake's lovely daughters had had the effect on me of a revelation of the human vitality, the creative force of flesh and blood, which is embodied in abstract thought" (160). Ideas matter greatly in this novel, but so do qualities, especially the "vitality" that animates Daisy herself, Grosbeake's daughters, and that is admired by pragmatic philosophy throughout the twenties. The daughters are muses of material ideas.

The novel has so far been a journey through a depressive American intellectual world bound tightly to the material culture around it. Like Fitzgerald in *The Great Gatsby*, Wilson uses a language of mechanism and commodities for feelings, which suggests that there really is no other choice: "As I went out to buy a bottle of gin at a nearby Italian restaurant, I resolved to disgorge all these ideas in a gigantic destructive essay. But I found now that I was getting a headache: my mind was still going on at a furious fatiguing rate—with slashed and deflated tyres, running rackingly on its rims—and I wanted now to make it stop" (133). Both novelists work with the now-dominant cultural image of the automobile. They are conscious, however, of new realities. A very few years after this was written, Freud would ironically describe technology that made man "a kind of prosthetic God."[27] Both Fitzgerald and Wilson use the automobile to suggest American entropy: the machines finally do run down. (Fitzgerald, however, is far more programmatic and really more skilled at dealing with facts and motifs. In *The Great Gatsby*, the automobile is part of action and experience. In Wilson it is a figure of speech.)

There is an understood connection between the narrator's state of mind and his models for thought. The Jamesian idea of will retains intellectual and even moral authority, but it has few possibilities for our own point in time. Wilson's subject was to be the recalcitrance of the mind, and, according to the narrator of *I Thought of Daisy*, we desire most of all unconsciousness. What is normal is "non-thinking and non-feeling," the mere metabolism of "bodily processes." The drift of consciousness that James described as a failure of self-direction we now understand to be the product of mental desires, and we are left "inertly drifting [this term has an intellectual history of its own] among random and meaningless images" (125). The concepts of drift and inertia imply not only the absence of will but of our national will to believe.[28] In fact, they restate William James's theory about "the spontaneous drift of thought," which habitually defeats our purposes. The mind—it is the American mind in James as in Wilson—has become indifferent to the powers of agency, reliant on the dim pleasures of unconsciousness. It is now unable "to keep affirming and adopting" thought, and to make it material.[29] Only that great cognate of vitality, "energy," can convert idea into being.

Late in life, Wilson reminded Arthur Schlesinger, Jr., that he had once edited Dewey, felt uneasy with his prose style, yet invested time in translating it. Before the publication of *I Thought of Daisy*, in what is arguably his most famous essay on American realities and ideals, Dewey had reorganized some of the basic tenets of pragmatism. One of them dovetailed with issues raised by Grosbeake-Whitehead: it was an attack on the kind of science based on principles rather than people. As Dewey put the matter, the measure of importance of any idea or consequence was its effect on "human interests." It was in fact a positive evil "when knowledge of nature is disconnected from its human function."[30] Like Whitehead, he wanted no separation of physics from that "human function." In 1930, Dewey published his opinion of American social character at its nadir in "Towards a New Individualism." And in that essay, he used exactly the same kind of language that Wilson had just used in *Daisy*: "Where is the wilderness which now beckons creative energy and affords untold opportunity and vigor? ... The wilderness exists in the movie and the novel; and the children of the pioneers ... enjoy pioneer life idly in the vicarious film. I see little social unrest which is the straining of energy for outlet in action. I find rather the protest against a weakening of vigor and a sapping of energy."[31] The display of energy is itself a value and makes other values contingent upon it. That is true in Jay Gatsby, in Myrtle Wilson, and also in Daisy, who knows that when you "keep using your vitality up" you become passive, inert, and can't "think about the situation" (183).

Related ideas come into play, and it is worth looking at Whitehead's text to see how vital thought works. The essays on "Symbolism" begin by observing that things "of a beautiful color and a beautiful shape" naturally arrest us. They have the capacity to act on "other elements of our experience." So, our response to things of beauty is never simply tropistic, but founded on the recognition of "the principle that symbolic reference holds between two components in a complex experience, each intrinsically capable of direct recognition."[32] That recognition needs a language to express it, but, "experience" being entirely "deceitful," the writer is well warned to consider the forms of expression. Any connection between idea and language begins with what Whitehead calls "presentational immediacy"—roughly equal to but a more advanced form of sense perception. The idea will be important to Wilson, who gets his warrant from Whitehead:

Presentational immediacy is our immediate perception of the contemporary external world, appearing as an element consti-

> tutive of our own experience. In this appearance the world discloses itself to be a community of actual things, which are actual in the same sense as we are.
>
> This appearance is effected by the mediation of qualities, such as colours, sounds, tastes, etc., which can with equal truth be described as our sensations or as the qualities of the actual things which we perceive.... The sense-data involved in presentational immediacy have a wider relationship in the world than these contemporary things can express.

Perception has its own values, and they are not insignificant, but it necessarily leads to the quality of "relatedness." That is to say, we ultimately recognize that "each concrete individual thing arises from its determinate relativity to the settled world of other concrete individuals."[33]

Reading *I Thought of Daisy* is the same as opening a set of *Matryoshkas*: Grosbeake talks about literature as it is understood according to Whitehead's symbolic logic, which then needs to be applied to Wilson's text as modified by other ideas from *Science and the Modern World*. We are well advised that Grosbeake, "aside from his appreciation of poetry, plays, and novels as such—which was in itself remarkable ... had also a brilliant faculty for reading into them social and moral history and revealing their philosophic implications" (157). In short, Whitehead may be said to precede us at our critical task.

The term "presentational immediacy" is derived from the "Presences of Nature" section of the first book of Wordsworth's *Prelude* (cited by Whitehead in the fifth chapter of *Science and the Modern World*). Arguing from romantic practice, Whitehead asserts that the depiction of nature by Wordsworth was necessarily also a "philosophy of nature." He adds that the "immediate presences of things" was Wordsworth's great interest, even obsession—understandable and necessary because presence first becomes idea, eventually relationship.[34] This section of *Science and the Modern World* is, I think, along with the essay on "Symbolism," the central source for Wilson's own theory.

The narrator of *I Thought of Daisy* tries throughout the Grosbeake episode to establish a connection between sensate images and human perceptions of them. Certain passages demand to be read through the overlay of *Science and the Modern World* and the "Symbolism" essay, especially those that refer to "colour," "shape," and "substance." (The first of these qualities is a constant in *any* of Whitehead's discussions of natural objects.) Whitehead's idea about the perception of essentials is exemplified by the dinner scene at his house, among his daughters. There are first of all things perceived by shape and function, especially the elaborate table furnishings. We see recognizably a cream pitcher, a sauceboat, saltcellars. But few things retain only their substantiality, and we are reminded of previous ideas and essences. To see these produced forms, all legs and handles, curves and surfaces, is to be reminded of their previous incarnations, and of the place of such things in memory. To look at them is to see the work "of Brueghel or Callot." They have a kind of second or demonic presence. Wilson adheres to the Whitehead vocabulary in calling attention to qualities that transcend materiality: "the colour and substance of the food seemed to have a special richness and density, as if they had been painted in a still-life" and the reds and whites have a "particularly lucent" quality that needs to be recalled (153). Color and substance imply memory and relationship.

Language and theory are transposed from Whitehead's essay. For example, in his opening pages Whitehead also conjures up an artist who represents the powers of perception. This artist has no special philosophical knowledge. But his sense of "beautiful colour" and "coloured shapes" leads him to understand that these things are inherently "symbols for some other elements in our experience." In Wilson's text, colors begin to imply ideas; they are in this section different from the rest of the novel in which desultory phrases ("a green carpet") make no connection to the mind. It is only after meeting Grosbeake that objects and their qualities take on complex meanings. The novel's language undergoes a transformation, becoming more intense and sensate, relying heavily on a new kind of imagery of "actual things," so that, for the first time, the "contemporary external world" can be perceived as it is.[35] Whitehead's essay invokes the artist; Wilson's passage also does, and invokes styles of depiction.

"Colour" and "substance," part of a still life here, are more extensively referential. Going forward, there is landscape in Wilson's notes on *The Forties:* "The big pond a wonderful deep dark green that reflected the pines of the banks in a deeper green than they were—it lay there embedded in the ground, a solid substance, absolutely smooth, absolutely motionless, with no watery vibration, not exactly vitreous, not exactly gelatinous, but like an unheard-of clear and rich mineral."[36] The passage, placing Wilson and his wife in the scene, is about love in a place he loves. But the language concerns more than symbolic denotation. Going backward—and for a long ways—we begin to detect the sources of Wilson's and of Whitehead's visual values: we are not, as William Hazlitt wrote, "to look in external nature for the form, the substance, the colour, the very life and being of whatever exists in our minds." The "true basis of metaphysical inquiry" is not physical fact but "consciousness, reflection . . . correspondent signs."[37] The repeated use of the terms "colour" and "substance" is far more definitive than a casual reading can reveal.

Intensity of description separates the whole Grosbeake section from the rest of the narrative. There is a sustained attempt to connect the presentational immediacy of this still life to other subjects. It has been preceded by a long view of the household and a close focus on Grosbeake's daughters. The narrator is in a room warmed and lit by fire. The objects in it have more than aesthetic valency: dark and grainy wood of great age, strong and heavy shapes, deep colors. Wilson uses a vocabulary of contour and color. But the most important thing to note may not involve form. These objects have their being, as Whitehead insisted, within the flow of time. What we see are spindles of English furniture "blacker and stronger-sinewed, as if they had been brought to a sharper focus, than American mahogany." The furniture is more functional and sharply focused than its American equivalent. Each of its attributes—grain and density, coloration and aging, reiterated closepacked drawers—implies "a tighter, compacter, and more downright civilization" (147).

There are some recognizable derivations. One of Whitehead's repeated points is the "enormous permanence" of nature.[38] Things not only are, but endure. A second and contingent point: there is a world of meaning "concealed" under appearances. Whatever we see is "heavy with the contact of the things gone by." That is a reasonable summation of Wilson's passage cited above. We recognize also the argument from Whitehead that "the present fact is luminously the outcome from its predecessors."[39] Like Dewey, Whitehead consistently argues that experience is a combination of what is undergone and understood. So, no object has mere spatial identity; all objects have their own history—involving ours. We are what we see.

The objects discerned exist within the flow of time and show its workings. Wilson's statement that metaphysics is the fiction of those who do not create concrete images has, I think, a corollary: concrete images imply metaphysics; and their use intuits metaphysics. The massed imagery of the Grosbeake section of the novel leads always toward some kind of synthesis. The array of English woods so much darker and heavier and more shapely than their counterparts are material forms of ideas, adding up to a concept of that agonistic term, "civilization." The passage continues with contrasting colors inescapably suggesting historical sequence, given the form containing their display. There is a historical sequence implied by close-connected color: pale autumn flowers, white ruffle-bordered curtains, and the additional patches substantiating a design that are contributed by "modernist paintings" on the walls.[40]

Back to the defining quality of color: in his seminal fifth chapter of *Science and the Modern World,* Whitehead remarks that "a colour is eternal. It haunts time like a spirit." He adds, "We are *within* a world of colours, sounds, and other sense-objects, related in space and time to enduring objects such as stones, trees, and human bodies." In "Symbolism, Its Meaning and Effect," he states that "coloured shapes seem to be symbols for some other elements in our experience." The concept of color leads to that of light, and Whitehead's examples of perception from romantic poetry are clustered around vision, sunlight, darkness, night, sky, "glittering" and "reflecting" surfaces.[41] Color is the most immediate thing normally perceived, initiating conceptual function on the part of the attentive viewer.

Wilson recognized the visual bias, adopted it, and organized his novel from the Grosbeake section to the end around reflected and ambient light. His language of light and color refers itself to—is a version of—the Whitehead theory:

> hair over her shoulders, like some spilling of gold . . . lightwaves . . . gazing out through the glass at the pavement lightly dappled with leaves and the dark grass glittering with wet . . . a vast crystal fixing its symmetry from a liquefied universe . . . iciness, glossy fall-leaf slivers and black rain-glinting glass . . . wires of ice, and tree branches decked with crystals. . . . The windows were orange against the snow, which was bluing and greying with the night . . . gold and black of a late November sunset . . . gigantic cracks of a light beyond human skies . . . fiery walls . . . a single yellow square of light . . . the moon, cut in brightest coldest silver over the lonely and frozen fields . . . the summer sun burned a blunt point of light, like the blinding violet-livid torch with which a worker on city mains gashes through a tough piece of pipe . . . vaporizing and fogging the air. . . . Assailed by the sunlight, we were dazed . . . in the brightness . . . sun streaked the water to the west with a bright glaze of zinc. . . . The colours had begun to come out on the vermilion smoke-stacks of steamers . . . the zinc-bright colourless sun. . . . We walked, dazed, up a little gangplank and down a very long white pier. . . . There were tiny children playing in the surf, in tiny slips of bathing-suits of yellow, pale green, and red, like the variously flavoured fruit-drops—orange, raspberry, and lime—in the glass jars we had passed on a candy counter. (159–93)

Whitehead has done the laboratory work; this is the field test. A set of responses has been triggered by laws of understanding as compelling as those of physics.[42] The last part of Wilson's novel is far more concerned with "presentational immediacy" than with the ideas about America that began the story. I should modify that: there will in fact be new ideas about America and the American self developing from the connection of things perceived. After pondering the aggregate of things seen under the aspect of Grosbeake's ideas, the Wilson narrator concludes that light and color "seemed to speak to me of bold and lonely thought" (163). To see a room full of objects is to specify that elusive quality of "civilization." To see Grosbeake and his wife is to reinforce the hope that "the body of humanity was invulnerably solid and sound" (156). Finally, the mass of images cited above shape themselves into a conclusion. The transit from Manhattan to Governor's Island to Staten Island to Coney Island is a kind of rebirth by water. It envisions something comparable to the ending of *The Great Gatsby*, in which place, moment, and idea merge for an instant: "I had been curiously moved by the sight of a single, solitary streetlamp on the Staten Island shore. It had merely shed a loose and whitish radiance over a few feet of the baldish road of some dark, thinly settled suburb. Above it, there had loomed an abundant and disorderly tree. *But there was America*" (emphasis added; 190). Each of Whitehead's six "notions" of natural philosophy—change, value, eternal objects, endurance, organism, interfusion—is necessarily present. But, the last, I think, intentionally dominates in order to convey the meaning of things so deeply interfused.

4

Reality's Thickness

Harry Levin's classic essay "What Was Modernism?" listed some of the defining works of the early twenties: *Ulysses, Sodome et Gomorrhe, The Waste Land, Jacob's Room,* and the *Later Poems* of Yeats. It explained modernism's connection to experimentalism, to the authority of mind, to evanescent time, to the new, urban spirit of place. It accounted for modernism's preeminence. But the essay is also an *apologia* for a literary movement no longer dominant. Levin saw two reasons for that: the first was the "uncompromising intellectuality" of modernists, which may have been too much for the middlebrow market to bear; the second was the gain of intellectual and even moral authority by science and the consequent loss of such authority by art. And yet, even science left much unanswered.

Toward the end of Levin's essay is an assertion followed by a question, both bound to be familiar to the reader of Edmund Wilson: science "has undergone a modernist phase of its own, and seen its solid premises subverted by such concepts as relativity and indeterminacy. Where, then, can we turn for illumination?"[1] Like Wilson, Levin invokes Alfred North Whitehead for the answer. Levin cites a passage of Wordsworth that was on Whitehead's mind: "If the labours of Men of science should ever create any material revolution, direct or indirect, in our condition, and in the impressions which we habitually receive, the Poet will sleep then no more than at present; he will be ready to follow the steps of the Man of science, not only in those general indirect effects, but he will be at his side, carrying sensation into the midst of the objects of the science itself."[2] That argument was sustained until mid-century. It circulated around the issue of reality: the way things actually were, the way they were perceived, the way that perception was stated. Above all was the conception of the thickness of reality, which meant that part of the world and of ourselves was not readily quantified, theorized, recognized.

Any complex version of reality required a sufficiently complex language. That being so, we might well ask another question about the twenties, "What Was Literature?" The decade began a steady production (and also restatement) of ideas about literature, particularly in defense of its powers of transmitting realities. Some of these ideas came from George Santayana, John Dewey, Walter Lippmann, and others outside the boundaries of fiction, not least of whom was William James. Hemingway was able to write about "thought" and "act" because of their work on experience, and because Whitehead and Wittgenstein had defined the difficult transition from experience to its literary statement. There was, however, bound to be a difference between instrumental and other forms of understanding. American philosophy sometimes used novels, plays, and poetry as exempla of the good life.[3] But, in a more sophisticated way, it identified the capacity of fiction to describe phenomena. One begins by understanding the mixed convictions of public philosophy and related thought from 1900 to 1930: literary statement was indispensable for its intuitive truth; it was a superior form of framing issues in dialogue; realism in fiction was highly suited to translating public into private issues; and, most important, philosophy might well learn from literature how to perceive natural properties and judge responses to them.

The impetus came from William James, as much a presence after his death as before.[4] In 1922, Robert H. Lowie, who contributed the "Science" chapter to *Civilization in the United States*, wrote that James was still influential, even dominant. He remained "far more than a great psychologist, philosopher, or literary man."[5] The 1925 Modern Library edition of *The Philosophy of William James* remade the point insistently. Edited by Horace M. Kallen, himself an intellectual figure until mid-century, it brought James to the modern and modernist audience. Kallen's preface states that this edition's "subjects . . . occupy the foreground of contemporary thought," among them, ideas of individual character and human relationship; knowledge and education; and the tangled issues of living in the American democracy. Kallen adds, possibly with asperity, that it was William James who knew more than anyone else about "the American temper and *the American scene*."[6] His introduction asserts that James was not merely the greatest of American philosophers (a disputed claim) but that he was universally understood to be "the great philosopher of America" (by no means an exaggeration).[7] Certain points raised by Kallen's summary are of substantive importance for my own theme: that experience is not reductive to principle, that it is insistently real despite the limits of human understanding; that "unpredictabilities" will always remain; and finally, that "truth and error are relations between things or events or ideas used as signs, symbols, or meanings."[8]

James understood literature to be both moral and intellectual, taking it, in other words, with the same seriousness as did Edmund Wilson and Harry Levin. In some cases literature provided moral guidance, but, more important, it made moral distinctions. Writing was itself a paradigm, revealing the will to affect inherent (and also supposed) limits of expressiveness. There were other, indispensable functions of literature. From James to Lionel Trilling it was understood that intellectual leadership under democracy depended on understanding texts that had worked out, in ways that the ordinary reader could not, the dilemmas of political and social life. And yet, it could never be a matter of direct transmission of values. There was an inherent political problem: democracy had not only to promote equality—which was morally satisfying and mentally deadening—but to create its own adversarial aristocracy of the mind. The terms were to change in the twenties, but the arguments remained. Here is James on the great problem of the "thought of my time":

> There is a passage in Darwin's short autobiography which has been often quoted.... "Up to the age of thirty or beyond it, poetry of many kinds gave me great pleasure; and even as a schoolboy I took intense delight in Shakespeare, especially in

the historical plays. I have also said that pictures formerly gave me considerable, and music very great delight. But now for many years I cannot endure to read a line of poetry. I have tried lately to read Shakespeare, and found it so intolerably dull that it nauseated me. I have also almost lost my taste for pictures or music. . . . My mind seems to have become a kind of machine for grinding general laws out of large collections of facts; but why this should have caused the atrophy of that part of the brain alone, on which the higher tastes depend, I cannot conceive. . . . The loss of these tastes is a loss of happiness, and may possibly be injurious to the intellect, and more probably to the moral character, by enfeebling the emotional part of our nature." We all intend when young to be all that may become a man, before the destroyer cuts us down. We wish and expect to enjoy poetry always, to grow more and more intelligent about pictures and music, to keep in touch with spiritual and religious ideas, and even not to let the greater philosophic thoughts of our time develop quite beyond our view. . . . [But] we make ourselves into Darwins in this negative respect by persistently ignoring the essential practical conditions of our case.[9]

The many references to literature in William James and also in John Dewey divide roughly into instrumental and experiential categories. The second category is more important, but the first has correspondences with the thought of Wilson, Levin, and also Lionel Trilling.[10] Characteristic of the first grouping is James's famous exhortation "The Social Value of the College-Bred" and his concluding chapter of *Pragmatism*. The former, like the passage on Darwin, admonishes the turn-of-the-century reader to brush up his Shakespeare, but it also argues that something called "criticism" is fundamentally important as an intellectual mode. It repeats the Jamesian theme that the texts of the humanities offer a useful parallel to scientific understanding. The passage on poetry in *Pragmatism* is highly prescriptive, and also highly sentimental, recommending the reading of a very long burst of Walt Whitman in order to become a better person. But, James observes,

"Verily a fine and moving poem, in any case, but there are two ways of taking it, both useful." The second way of taking it "suggests an infinitely larger number of the details of future experience to our mind."[11]

James anticipates Whitehead on the superiority of literary language for describing phenomena, especially in three essays ("Concerning Fechner," "The Compounding of Consciousness," and "Bergson and Intellectualism") from *A Pluralistic Universe*. The first of these won't win converts to the theory of a world-totality of consciousness that includes the "feeling-life of plants." It is James in his late phase of metaphysical idealism. But, it does crystallize James's ideas about the language of scientific statement. Gustave Theodor Fechner influenced James on this and certain other issues because he worked both in the sciences and the humanities, or at the "cross-roads of truth." Immensely productive, Fechner spent his life pursuing both intuitive and scientific patterns of reasoning. James was particularly struck by Fechner's recognition of the abstract in the concrete, a conception as close to the idea of imagism as may be imagined before Pound. Fechner's lyricism allowed him to apply the resources of poetic language to the description of landscape. That language was considerably more complex and nuanced than its scientific equivalent. Here is how James puts the issue of perception/description of phenomena: "absolute idealism, thinking of reality only under intellectual forms, knows not what to do with *bodies* of any grade, and can make no use of any psychophysical analogy or correspondence."[12] It is difficult, perhaps impossible, to go along with James or Fechner when they argue for the ideal of world-consciousness, but there is something of lasting importance to the view that "perceptive experiences" and "visual sensation" need to be expressed in a language larger than that of either science or philosophy. Henri Bergson mattered to James because he had mastered the meaning of "the perceptual flux which the conceptual translation so fatally leaves out." James took from Bergson the view that thought "deals thus solely with surfaces. It can name the thickness of reality, but it cannot fathom it." There are good reasons why the following should be familiar:

> The only way in which to apprehend reality's thickness is either to experience it directly by being a part of reality one's self, or

to evoke it in imagination by sympathetically divining some one else's inner life. . . . If what we care most about be the synoptic treatment of phenomena, the vision of the far and the gathering of the scattered like, we must follow the conceptual method. But if, as metaphysicians, we are more curious about the inner nature of reality or about what really makes it go, we must turn our backs upon our winged concepts altogether, and bury ourselves in the thickness of those passing moments.[13]

There is a triangular relationship between this statement, Henry James's critical comments in his life of Hawthorne, and Lionel Trilling's recurrent use of its language and idea. The concept of "reality's thickness" had yet some time and distance to evolve.

John Dewey took up the subject of poetic statement in his aesthetics, but the most important of his arguments about literature are, I think, in his essays on experience. His best-known essay on social philosophy, "Search for the Great Community," ends with an outline of the meaning of "literary presentation." Here is Dewey on the perception and interpretation of phenomena:

> Presentation is fundamentally important, and presentation is a question of art. . . . Men's conscious life of opinion and judgment often proceeds on a superficial and trivial plane. But their lives reach a deeper level. The function of art has always been to break through the crust of conventionalized and routine consciousness. Common things, a flower, a gleam of moonlight, the song of a bird, not things rare and remote, are means with which the deeper levels of life are touched so that they spring up as desire and thought. This process is art. Poetry, the drama, the novel, are proofs that the problem of presentation is not insoluble. Artists have always been the real purveyors of news, for it is not the outward happening in itself which is new, but the kindling by it of emotion, perception and appreciation.[14]

"Presentation," the term coined by Wordsworth, revived by Whitehead, rediscovered by Edmund Wilson, is used here to make a related point about the description of things and feelings. Dewey respected ideas that could not be explored solely through analysis, and thought that they were often to be located in lyrical statement. Dewey's theory of experience begins with the conception that it is based on fact but is not fact itself and does not rest on fact alone. We are reminded of Hemingway's contemporaneous idea that truth is best stated by fiction. As for Dewey, only when experience becomes language can it be comprehended, hence the importance of the sole mode concerned with that process. Dewey adds to the discussion of lyric the value of "perception" as well as that of "emotion," implying the accurate recovery of experience through art. In his realm, that was a possibility.

Dewey's essay on Henry Adams, John Keats, and Walter Pater praises the last of these great figures for the idea that "the sensible world" can be detected through "sensuous images." He cites Pater's observation that "the elevation of the ideal above and beyond immediate sense has operated not only to make it pallid and bloodless, but it has acted, like a conspirator with the sensual mind, to impoverish and degrade all things of direct experience."[15] The citation reminds us not only of Dewey's grounds of criticism, but of the presence of Pater in later literary-critical thought. Dewey's locus classicus of 1929 continues the association between literature and reality:

> Philosophic discourse partakes both of scientific and literary discourse. Like literature, it is a comment on nature and life in the interest of a more intense and just appreciation of the meanings present in experience. Its business is reportorial and transcriptive only in the sense in which the drama and poetry have that office. Its primary concern is to clarify, liberate and extend the goods which inhere in the naturally generated functions of experience. It has no call to create a world of "reality" *de novo,* nor to delve into secrets of Being hidden from common-sense and science. . . . It departs from the arts of literary discourse. They have a freer office to perform—to perpetuate, enhance and vivify in imagination the natural goods.[16]

Alan Ryan observes of Dewey's partiality for literature that although the world is not *"literally* a text to be read," we must learn to "read" it so.[17] It was Dewey's habit to find meaning in verse, and also to imitate its statement of meaning. One is grateful for the account of Dewey's own poetry on reality—written with emotion, crumpled in his desk drawer, thrown away in his wastebasket, found by the janitor, published by his widow. That poetry imitated Wordsworth, Dewey's final authority on nature.[18] But mechanism intervened: Dewey wrote that "we must bridge this gap of poetry from science. We must heal this unnatural wound. We must in the cold, reflective way of critical system, justify and organize the truth which poetry, with its quick, naive contacts, has already felt and reported."[19]

These are important points, but perhaps the most important of them is the conviction that language was the "tool of tools" for the understanding of phenomena. In fact, organic nature and its responses—"pains, pleasures, odors, colors, noises, tones"—could not be understood without it.[20] Dewey's tastes ran toward romanticism and Victorian lyric, and for that he was roundly dismissed by writers like Van Wyck Brooks, but he understood an essential aspect of modernism: words were inherently experimental; meanings combine, shift, and change; experience undergoes, in his phrase, a kind of "transubstantiation" through language.[21]

These ideas about coming to terms with reality were to affect Edmund Wilson and Lionel Trilling. The sequel took some time to unfold. In 1931, Edmund Wilson began *Axel's Castle* by observing that literature had undergone two revolutions: the first, its liberation from Cartesian logic by romanticism; the second, the advent of symbolism. Throughout, Wilson argued that the issue was the understanding of reality: the first task of writing was clearly to "correspond to actual experience." But it was impossible to account for experience through the laws of mechanics, "things as they really are" demanding the complexity of a different explanatory mode. Wilson used a terminology of theoretical disconnection and mental indistinctness—"complicated," "turbulent," "insubordinate," "vaporous," "turbid," "indefiniteness" and, especially, "confusion"—to imply the escape of the actual event from its formulation.[22] That is what Fitzgerald did in *The Great Gatsby,* and possibly the mentor learned from the student.

Wilson understood symbolism to be the primary mode for understanding the thickness of reality. One Wilsonian phrase—"our sensations as we actually experience them"—is from the opening chapter of *Axel's Castle* but might have come from anywhere in the experiential essays of James or Dewey.[23] Certainly, James's conception of "the abstract in the concrete" underlies Wilson's ideas in general, and in particular his analysis of Paul Valéry, whose "poetry is then always shifting back and forth between this palpable and visible world and a realm of intellectual abstraction."[24] Wilson understood Valéry's work to be at the intersection of his own ideas on science, literature, and reality:

> Will the sciences dominate the future, as Pierre de Massot has suggested in a book which traces the development of Symbolism from Mallarmé to Dadaism, "smothering the last works of the past, until the day when literature, music and painting have become the three principal branches of neurology?" Paul Valéry has recently predicted that as radio, moving pictures and television come to take the place of books as means of affecting people's feelings and ideas, literature, as we have known it in the past, may become "as obsolete and as far removed from life and practice as geomancy, the heraldic art and the science of falconry." Literature, according to Valéry, has become "an art which is based on the *abuse of language*—that is, it is based on language as a creator of illusions, and not on language as a means of transmitting realities."[25]

The conflict between recognizing the nature of reality and transmitting reality engaged Wilson in a number of ways. Leon Edel says of Wilson's dilemma in the period 1926–1930 (the period not only of *Axel's Castle* and *I Thought of Daisy* but of his encounter with Whitehead's *Science and the Modern World* and the essays on symbolic logic): "Could a work of art, the world filtered through the mind of an individual, still be 'reality,' once it receives the imprint and color of that mind?"[26] So far as Wilson was concerned, it could not. "Literature and art," he writes, "cannot truly represent life" because they are the consequence of extreme self-consciousness. They impose the author's feelings—which in his own case he found unreliable—on his subject.

Wilson went so far as to state that "all of literature gives a false view of life, because it is the obverse of the reality." That was the subjective problem, but there was a scientific, objective problem as well. It was impossible to recover the atomic nature of experience because of the flow of reaction within infinite units of (necessarily) unrecorded time. Necessarily, "the artist fills in the holes" with the connective tissue of "fabrication."[27]

Even when free of the laws of mechanics the mind was subject to other limitations. Wilson believed that there was a tremendous discrepancy between "the self which experiences and the self which writes." He rejected one aspect of romanticism, the conception that emotion *could* be recollected in tranquility. There was, he thought, absolutely no connection between experienced moments of pain and their reconstruction by the conscious mind.[28] Wilson was a radical convert to the philosophy of experience, believing for a time that each poet required his own symbolic language because it was the nature of experience to be so fleeting and vague that it really could not otherwise be conveyed. It was a position due to be modified, and it was by the time of his essay on "The Dream of H. C. Earwicker" in *The Wound and the Bow*. But, he alternated between taking comfort from the assurances of Whitehead that the language of literature might suffice, and his own anxious, even depressive conviction that such language might not be capable of "transubstantiation," or of translation. He may have been depressive, but he was in some respects right.

I have more confidence in his argument than in the counter-argument raised by the biologist Edward O. Wilson. He claims that Edmund Wilson was an early defender of the idea of consilience or the replication of the physical sciences in literature.[29] This comes from a limited reading of the texts and a limited, Cartesian understanding of the subject. E. O. Wilson states that there can be a "reconstitution" of outer reality in our minds; the problem is only that of aligning "sensory input" with our own conceptual process. Improvements in the understanding of neural circuits will then result in our complete recognition of external reality.[30] Even if this were true for perception, which is doubtful, this theory would disregard nearly all of the other intellectual work of writing, notably the enormous problem of statement. And that is to say nothing of the conceptual-linguistic difficulties argued by Wittgenstein. Edmund Wilson was concerned with what writing does, and also how it is prevented from the accomplishment by the mind's own interposition.

The idea of objectivity to which Edward O. Wilson appeals was in fact dispelled before he stated it. Lionel Trilling, in the first annual Jefferson Lecture, reviewed the literary-philosophical evidence on objective statement and concluded that such statement "can never wholly succeed." That, he added, "is guaranteed by the nature of individual persons, by the nature of society, even, the philosophers tell us, by the nature of the mind itself."[31] He analyzes the problem at length elsewhere,[32] reminding us that Jane Austen's *Mansfield Park* argues explicitly against the idea that anything—"whatever were to be expressed"—can find statement sufficiently true, i.e., uncolored by personal involvement or valuation or conception. The argument that reality can be fully expressed through words has been subverted by writers like Jane Austen—to read these writers is to realize that Ludwig Wittgenstein had much to work with.

Questions about reality are at the heart of *The Twenties*. According to Leon Edel, Edmund Wilson was haunted by the belief that literature *falsified* reality. That is to say, he could not accept the view of James and Dewey that literature was the great mode of reconstructing experience. There were too many obstacles, chief among them authorial subjectivity and the obsessive "ordering of the disorderly," which is part of writing itself.[33] The longest, most complex of Wilson's journal entries amplifies the problem of that "great Whiteheadian organism" whose thought produces art.[34] First, the nature of the event itself: "Don't forget history.... When things happen, they do not seem to happen in the world of literature—except in that cultivated conversation which is a form of literature—but in a barbarous animal world, bloody, ignoble, uncontrollable." Second, after things happen, they are reimagined. Third, both Russell and Whitehead have already shown that logic is limited by paradox, and that it may be impossible "for ordinary language to handle" the proliferation of ideas. Fourth, the often reiterated point that "the turbid chaos of life" resists the ordering impulse of literature. Fifth, a kind of principle of "Incommensurability" that is inherent in the attempt of one entity to judge another, as in the attempt "of the critics of the school of Eliot, with their horror of politics, propaganda, popularity and journalism" who descend into their own troubled form of philosophical abstraction. The consequence of these things is that literature is only "the result of our rude collisions with reality." It does the wrong things, explaining, justifying, harmonizing, and ordering against the evidence that life is fundamentally indecipherable.[35]

Lionel Trilling did not believe that life was indecipherable—quite the opposite. He thought that literature was the essential mode of moral and analytical understanding. But he too was concerned with the limits of interpretation, and he extended the particular idea of reality's thickness. Trilling was highly conscious of the work of William James, regarding him as a defining figure who had articulated the central issue of modern times: the conflict between will and necessity. He admired James's act of recognition that "*something* demanded of him the exercise of his will and that therefore his ego had the traditional evidence that it was actual." As Trilling saw it, James was clearly in the right: "The careful balance between will and necessity which the nineteenth century undertook to maintain was no mere psychological construct. It reflected realities of the culture."[36]

The main issue for Trilling was the way the mind works against nature and culture. For this, William James was essential. Quite early on, in *Matthew Arnold* (which is a book of the late thirties), Trilling began a long series of references to the Jamesian philosophy. He begins by noting the seriousness with which he takes James's work on mental conflict.[37] But this is only groundwork. Trilling finds that "the chaotic flux of thought, the multifariousness of impression, the unceasing creative combinations unconsciously made" need a certain kind of philosophy to describe them, even if they cannot be explained. And he uses the great Jamesian phrase of a "continuous flow of the mental stream" to make his point.[38] Trilling wrote an intuitive passage on the relationship of James and Arnold, and then a long comparison of the two on the problem of what he called "extradition," or the difficulty of objectifying the "subjective state."[39] A major amount of *Matthew Arnold* is necessarily devoted to the psychology of religion, and it is William James whom Trilling chooses to illuminate alternatives. (It is important to note that Trilling has a long list of philosophers to draw on, from Spinoza to Santayana.[40]) In short, from the beginning of his professional life Trilling was absorbed by the answers proposed by William James to the problem of stating subjective experience in an objective way.

Later, in "Manners, Morals, and the Novel," Trilling addressed directly that "thick social texture" so brilliantly outlined by Henry James in his life of Hawthorne. James meant the almost infinite layering of institutions, classes, and rituals that make up culture and enable it to be depicted. But Trilling kept on using and reinvoking the phrase, moving it beyond its original boundaries. He went first to the conception of life having "increasingly thickened" in America after James; then to the kind of thickening that Balzac understood, a matter not so much of having an endless list of sub-societies to describe but of understanding complex, many-layered, contradictory reality.[41] And Trilling did indeed combine the two terminologies, writing about "thickness" in exactly the same way that William James and Dewey had used the idea, and aiming it at the conception of "reality" he had inherited:

> When, generations from now, the historian of our times undertakes to describe the assumptions of our culture, he will surely discover that the word *reality* is of central importance in his understanding of us. He will observe that for some of our philosophers the meaning of the word was a good deal in doubt, but that for our political writers, for many of our literary critics, and for most of our reading public, the word did not open discussion but, rather, closed it. Reality, as conceived by us, is whatever is external and hard, gross, unpleasant. Involved in its meaning is the idea of power conceived in a particular way. Some time ago I had occasion to remark how, in the critical estimates of Theodore Dreiser, it is always being said that Dreiser has many faults but that it cannot be denied that he has great power. No one ever says "a kind of power." Power is assumed to be always "brute" power, crude, ugly, and undiscriminating, the way an elephant appears to be. It is seldom understood to be the way an elephant actually is, precise and

discriminating; or the way electricity is, swift and absolute and scarcely embodied.[42]

Trilling proceeds from a discussion of Henry James, but he silently moves into the territory of William James. He mentions the concept of "reality" because it had so recently engaged Bergson, Bradley, James, Dewey, and others. Trilling is engaged in a large project, one which has, I think, evaded the attention of those who followed him, and it is that of understanding philosophical and scientific connotations of literary criticism. James, Dewey, and Wilson thought about reality as an infinitely expanded form of what was merely visible. This fit in with scientific observation, but there was something Platonic in their engagement with it. Reality signified the immense, uncountable complexities of objects multiplied by those of perceptions to constitute a realm of experience beyond the power of quantification. One hoped that literature could clarify the problem. But, the evidence of modernist literature was precisely the inability of language to state at any given time that reality had been captured, formulated, and pinned to a wall. Trilling introduced this passage with a certain phrase: "*in a time like this* what we need is reality in large doses." It is an allusion; he has just plainly stated that some forms of fiction and criticism might be neither "literature" nor "reality." Trilling follows in the path of James and Dewey: statement fails to become literature by imitating science, finding single meanings in experience, limiting itself to naturalism, or becoming politics. It is important to note that Trilling's proofs were anchored to Fitzgerald and Hemingway. In his 1939 essay "Hemingway and His Critics," Trilling argues that a complex theory of reality is almost never *desired* by criticism. He values Hemingway because he asserted values independent of and invulnerable to orthodoxy: "For upon Hemingway were turned all the fine social feelings of the now passing decade, all the noble sentiments, all the desperate optimism, all the extreme rationalism, all the contempt of irony and indirection—all the attitudes which, in the full tide of the liberal-radical movement, became dominant in our thought about literature. There was demanded of him earnestness and pity, social consciousness, as it was called, something 'positive' and 'constructive' and literal. For is not life a simple thing and is not the writer a villain or a counterrevolutionary who does not see it so?"[43]

Trilling retains the ideas of Dewey and James. In "Manners, Morals, and the Novel" he invokes their terminology:

> The word *reality* is an honorific word and the future historian will naturally try to discover our notion of its pejorative opposite, appearance, mere appearance. He will find it in our feeling about the internal; whenever we detect evidences of style and thought we suspect that reality is being a little betrayed, that "mere subjectivity" is creeping in. There follows from this our feeling about complication, modulation, personal idiosyncrasy, and about social forms, both the great and the small. . . . We claim that the great advantage of reality is its hard, bedrock, concrete quality, yet everything we say about it tends toward the abstract and it almost seems that what we want to find in reality is abstraction itself. Thus we believe that one of the unpleasant bedrock facts is social class, but we become extremely impatient if ever we are told that social class is indeed so real that it produces actual differences of personality.[44]

The point for James especially had been that not all abstractions can be plotted on some kind of intellectual navigation chart. Trilling has unerringly concentrated on an argument derived from another kind of perception and used its conclusions: the concrete fact or thing or object or "reality" does *not* lead us to a single conclusion or idea. The language of reality is unfixed, even the same image or word having different meanings at different times. When those philosophers who have just been invoked by Trilling consider the aptness of poetic language they never state that it is finite, only that it is different. Trilling ends this long passage with an allusion to what he believes is the most telling of proofs, returning to Fitzgerald's astonishing sense of difference in sameness, individuation within class. The theme is beautifully developed in Trilling's essay on Fitzgerald that takes its point of departure from the novelist's own ambiguity. The point was Fitzgerald's precise "social observation" of the complex and sometimes irreducible "actuality of personal life."[45] Individual things and persons—i.e., the "very rich"—are never generic. In other words, Fitzgerald, like Hemingway, has both social and phenomenological credibility.

The idea of "thickness," or unknowable complication, is everywhere in Trilling's essays. He writes that "reality is always material reality," i.e., that even intellectual life in America wants badly to reduce causation and relationship, to be free of doubt. That became in his lifetime a political necessity because all that is "doctrinaire" aspires to prediction, not discovery.[46] He was famously an admirer of Freud, but even in Freud he noted self-imposed limits of "simple materialism" and "simple determinism." That, Trilling argues, is Freud's central weakness, his inability to understand art that cannot be reduced by explanation, utilized to make the ego more independent of the superego, and finally to replace the untold variousness of the id by a single logic of control. (Trilling states, correctly enough, that "pragmatism is anathema to Freud through the greater part of his intellectual career.") But art should refuse to work within the limits of that "rationalistic positivism" that prevented thinkers like Freud from understading complex reality.[47] Perhaps the best place for me to end a study that has been so centrally concerned with the idea of scientific and literary realities is with Trilling's own summation in "The Princess Casamassima":

> There is always the defense to be made that the special job of literature is, as Marianne Moore puts it, the creation of "imaginary gardens with real toads in them." The reader who detects that the garden is imaginary should not be led by his discovery to a wrong view of the reality of the toads. In settling questions of reality and truth in fiction, it must be remembered that, although the novel in certain of its forms resembles the accumulative and classificatory sciences, which are the sciences most people are at home with, in certain other forms the novel approximates the sciences of experiment.[48]

Trilling concludes by reminding the reader that reality is ambiguous, as is the imagination. But the essay is so full of themes from William James and Dewey—themes of comparative scientific and literary understanding, of the meaning of consciousness, of the variousness that cannot be confined to ascription, of probability and, above all, of the complex idea of reality's thickness—that it must stand as one of the last statements of an extraordinarily open and modulated American philosophy.

◄ 5 ►

Hemingway's Plain Language

In 1922, in his introduction to the *Tractatus* of Ludwig Wittgenstein, Bertrand Russell wrote that "the essential business of language is to assert or deny facts.... In order that a certain sentence should assert a certain fact there must, however the language may be constructed, be something in common between the structure of the sentence and the structure of the fact."[1] Like Wittgenstein, he was concerned with intellectual honesty, believing that in the new marketplace of ideas words might no longer "have a connection of one sort or another with facts."[2] We often accept that Hemingway's use of language corresponds to the relationship drawn by Bertrand Russell, that its simplicity implies the faithful transcribing of fact rather than the more ambiguous process of interpreting or changing reality.

However, the problem of accurate statement was much debated during and after the twenties. It was concluded, often by reference to the work of Whitehead and to that of Wittgenstein, that clarity in the form of fidelity to experience may be unattainable. Those who thought about language in the twenties realized that it might not after all relate to facts. There were many reasons, among them that during the interval between the experienced fact and its recollection too many variables had been introduced.[3] In any case, Wittgenstein argued convincingly then and later that language was often a barrier to the expression of thought, which may not progress at all, or even turn out to be circular—a kind of "infinite regress."[4]

Hemingway largely agreed: the last chapter of *The Sun Also Rises* reminds Brett when she tries to assess her experience with Romero that "you'll lose it if you talk about it."[5] The novel reflects often on the inability of language to state reality, recall feeling, replicate (or even approach) experience. In the first of the following passages, Count Mippipopolous urges the unwilling Brett to talk about herself; in the second, he avoids answering questions about his wounds; in the third, at a later moment in the story, Jake describes the friendship between aficionados at Montoya's. In no case is it possible to trust even one's own language:

> "Why don't you just talk?"
> "I've talked too ruddy much. I've talked myself all out to Jake."
> "I should like to hear you really talk, my dear. When you talk to me you never finish your sentences at all."
> "Leave 'em for you to finish. Let any one finish them as they like."
> "It is a very interesting system." (58)

> The count was tucking in his shirt.
> "Where did you get those?" I asked.
> "In Abyssinia. When I was twenty-one years old."
> "What were you doing?" asked Brett. "Were you in the army?"
> "I was on a business trip, my dear."
> "I told you he was one of us. Didn't I?" Brett turned to me. "I love you, count. You're a darling." (60)

> There was no password, no set questions that could bring it out, rather it was a sort of oral spiritual examination. (132)

Brett may have more "system" than appears: *The Sun Also Rises* was published four years after Russell wrote that "a certain sentence" should "assert a certain fact." The first passage cited argues the opposite. Brett understands that language is not adequate to the case. Her judgment is widely shared: we now accept that "the very possibility of a consistent use of the expression 'true sentence' which is in harmony with the laws of logic and the spirit of everyday language seems to be very questionable."[6] In order to discuss the subject she would have to conceal or lie; there is no possibility of *anyone* stating a "true sentence" on that subject. In terms of character, Brett has flaws, but false idealism is not among them. In terms of narrative, we begin to understand that there are reasons for silence throughout. In terms of context, Hemingway begins to argue that statement and fact are disconnected because they reflect the disorder of reality.

If anything, the Count is converted by Brett's silent honesty; he in turn wins *her* admiration by refusing to explain his early life. That is not because he has had an immoral life, only that it would be immoral to talk about it. Language falsifies. The last passage reminds us, as Donald Davidson has put the issue, that meanings are so difficult to inscribe that it may be necessary to know a person's belief before knowing what his statements mean.[7] That may usefully be applied to the second passage, in which to know that the Count is "one of us"—a phrase repeated—is to know after all what is essential. Hemingway's language is full of ideas about language.

There is more than one problem of statement. The first is that Hemingway and other modernists value directness and simplicity, understanding that they express complexity; the second concerns expression itself. Wittgenstein had recognized many cases in which we could not even know what we perceive, and he had made the famous observation that silence was best when dealing with those many things that remain unknowable. And Bergson had endowed modernism with this view—it complements Wittgenstein—of words themselves: "Not only does language make us believe in the unchangeableness of our sensations, but it will sometimes deceive us as to the nature of the sensation felt. . . . In short, the word with well-defined outlines, the rough and ready word, which stores up the stable, common, and consequently impersonal element in the impressions of mankind, overwhelms or at least covers over the delicate and fugitive impressions of our individual consciousness." Words, as soon as they are formed, "turn against the sensation which gave birth to them."[8] That last is an elegant paraphrase of Brett's reason for silence. She is a larger presence than may appear.

Like all writers, Hemingway was affected by contemporary ideas. I think that he had the Wittgenstein cast of mind, although we associate him with the Russell cast of mind.[9] A recent essay by Louis Sass—it is of exceptional quality—examines in particular the relationship of Wittgenstein's ideas to the arts. It is of primary importance to balance the demands of others who are witness to our lives against the exigencies of the honest self. It follows from Wittgenstein that the honest self refuses moralizing and even explanation. Theatricality or self-explanation is "a loss of personal integrity"—as well as a diminishment of one's own existence. Is Brett a weak self, composed, as rather a lot of critics have suggested, of nothing more than alcohol, self-pity, and sexuality? Or is she an authentic self as intuited by Wittgenstein, secure enough to give up language because it is insufficient to the case? Wittgenstein preferred literature, according to Sass, which refused to compromise experience by explanation, i.e., "by attempting to say what can only be shown." In fact, he endowed modernism with a kind of "premise of unspeakability." One avoids corrupting experience by wrongly describing it.[10]

It is rare for Hemingway to suggest that perception can be captured by language. He thought about the possibility, and it did once happen at "a good cafe . . . on the Place St.-Michel":

> A girl came in the cafe and sat by herself at a table near the window. She was very pretty with a face fresh as a newly minted coin if they minted coins in smooth flesh with rain-freshened skin, and her hair was black as a crow's wing and cut sharply and diagonally across her cheek. I looked at her and she disturbed me and made me very excited. I wished I could put her in the story, or anywhere, but she had placed herself so she could watch the street and the entry and I knew she was waiting for someone. So I went on writing.
>
> The story was writing itself and I was having a hard time keeping up with it. I ordered another rum St. James and I watched the girl whenever I looked up, or when I sharpened the pencil with a pencil sharpener with the shavings curling into the saucer under my drink. I've seen you, beauty, and you

belong to me now, whoever you are waiting for and if I never see you again, I thought. You belong to me and all Paris belongs to me and I belong to this notebook and this pencil.[11]

The passage is a paradigm of realism, and it suggests why Hemingway has become an icon of mass culture. It responds to the demand for art as replication. The visual values of the subject have been rendered without reference to much else; she is now an image waiting to be recalled. Description depends silently on the analogy of writing and the visual arts, an analogy driven too far. But when Hemingway is less ego-driven, he is on the other side of the issue, consistently warning the reader that language does not express thought, much less "capture" reality. In fact, he will argue that language is not reconstruction but a new reality itself.[12]

Intensely sympathetic to the problems of literary statement, John Dewey wrote in 1925 that philosophy, science, and literature all shared certain characteristics, chief among them "reportorial and transcriptive" functions. Literature, however, had a special function in addition: "to create a world of 'reality' *de novo*." That was why Dewey in his essays on experience addressed writers like Keats, Pater, Henry Adams, and Wordsworth. And why he kept up-to-date with lesser figures like W. H. Hudson, who seemed to illuminate certain issues such as the escape from artificial culture into authentic primitivism. Dewey hoped to find what Marianne Moore would call the real toad in the garden of fiction, i.e., truth imagined.[13] So did Whitehead, although less benevolently: "Language is incomplete and fragmentary, and merely registers a stage in the average advance beyond ape-mentality. But all men enjoy flashes of insight beyond meanings already stabilized in etymology and grammar. Hence the role of literature."[14] It was fair enough: a warning that fiction tells only a kind of truth.

In Hemingway we see the author's sense of the difficulty of turning perception and experience into language, and the problem that his characters have, for a variety of reasons, in stating their own feelings and meanings. Those characters will often resist statement, or state things that they know are disconnected from fact.

There is a well-defined scene that suggests meanings beyond dialogue. In the sixth chapter of *The Sun Also Rises,* Jake Barnes approaches an outside table at the Select where Harvey Stone is drinking. Stone is broke, a drunk who hasn't eaten in five days by his own count, but he seems to understand a good deal: that Mencken has written about all the things he knows and is now working on all the things he doesn't; and that "He's through now"—an accurate statement for 1926. He also knows that Robert Cohn, who has just entered, is a case of arrested development, which the preceding chapters have suggested but not put so precisely. Cohn blusters, threatens him, then finally gives up when Stone says, "It doesn't make any difference to me. You don't mean anything to me." Given Cohn's cast of mind, which is what the scene is about, it is the ultimate offense. When Stone gets up to leave, after saying everything about Cohn that is necessary to understand his part in the book, Jake watches him "crossing the street through the taxis, small, heavy, slowly sure of himself in the traffic" (42–44).

Stone is one of those laconic presences in Hemingway who transmit ideas without wasting much language on them. We see him in a recurrent location—it is a *querencia*—used again by Hemingway in this novel and also in "A Clean, Well-Lighted Place," "The Undefeated," and a number of other stories.[15] Hemingway's scenes at bars and cafes have no social dimension, and often appear, because of that, to be allegorical. Everything takes place in the present. Character is reductive, and very little attention is paid to human attachments. Ideas and other concerns seem to be disturbances in the way of meaningful silence. Harvey Stone (or Harold E. Stearns on whom he is based) might well have deserved development because his life was so intelligent and self-destructive. He was in many ways like Fitzgerald, beginning the literary life high, falling low, ending soon. But Hemingway is not interested here in his being a *figura* of the twenties.[16]

The bar or cafe scene strips things to their essentials. But there is a trap set for the critic because the essential may not be verbal, or entirely visible. The nonverbal elements of these scenes matter as much as dialogue, and one needs to note silence as a value, even as an intellectual value. The scene with Harvey Stone has him in its center; he is not a perceived object. The conversation goes as he determines. There is nothing intervening between statement and judgment, which Cohn finds distressing, but which Barnes admires. Like the old man in "A Clean, Well-Lighted Place," Stone is a kind of immovable object.

As for language in these kinds of scenes, plain monosyllables may not denote, instead they invite translation. They need the latter because dialogue may encode its own subject. This particular scene develops an unmistakable tendency in its dialogue, but it works because Cohn's words break on Stone's presence.

The language of such scenes is plain. But, in another cafe scene, this one in the sixteenth chapter of *The Sun Also Rises,* the use of language is ambiguous. This scene shows Jake more or less delivering Brett to Romero. Issues here are far less direct, and almost no line in the dialogue refers to its own denoted meaning. Instead, each line suggests its own displacement by some other unspoken line, which the reader needs to provide. Even plain language has its complications: Brett has already warned us (it is vulgate Wittgenstein) that "talking's all bilge" (55).

This part of the chapter (184–87) begins with Brett asking Jake to get Romero to come to her. Almost nothing that follows depends on stated meanings. As the text itself suggests more than once, what is stated is disguised. Style, tone, and "manners" are going to matter; and at all times the respondent (and also the reader) will need to interpret meanings or even provide them.[17] All the characters in the dialogue keep reminding themselves of this. We are given a number of explicit warnings about the difference between meaning and statement. Here, Romero is drawn to their table, an act described with the deceptive clarity of crossing terrain, but there is necessarily a subtext: in *A Farewell to Arms,* which is more open about motive, Rinaldi remarks that Frederic Henry, who has also been attracted to a woman, has "that pleasant air of a dog in heat."[18] It may be that one text can usefully imply the other.

Romero "was being very careful. I think he was sure, but he did not want to make any mistake." When a fictional character needs to interpret meanings, the line reminds the reader to do the same. Recent Hemingway studies remind us that, "obtaining the complete facts of objective reality, if such a thing exists, is both crucial and impossible."[19] It certainly must have seemed so for Whitehead, who wrote in *Science and the Modern World* (1925) that "The total temporal duration of . . . an event bearing an enduring pattern constitutes its *specious present*."[20] That last phrase is endlessly complex but it does allow us to make sense of many passages in Hemingway, especially those cited here. Whitehead goes on to argue that the "specious present" encourages us to think that we can capture the reality of a moment, but that the idea is impossible to sustain because there are always other subjects embedded in our previous experience that bias the interpretation of whatever follows them.

This particular passage suggests how hard it is to deal with an event in that "specious present," in which everything rests on interpretation, and also on other events in our memory that are similar to the one being experienced and that prepare us for thinking in parallel. Is Romero careful because his own friends on the other side of the cafe are hostile witnesses? Does he respond uneasily to the sexually charged situation? Is it that his assertion of "authority" over another male needs to be just right? He may sense that his authority is not going to sway Brett—quite the opposite. Is he careful because he recognizes the opéra-bouffe aspect of the triangle and wants what he wants without demeaning himself to get it? Is the "mistake" of manners only? Probably not. Jake says, "He must have felt it when Brett gave him her hand." It is a heavy and usefully indeterminate line, suggesting that dialogue, itself a mask, requires some added form of perception.

In *The Red and the Black,* Julien Sorel experiences a sexual awakening and its possibility by holding a woman's hand. It is a great erotic moment. Hemingway will often stage his own revivals, reminding the reader of Flaubert's carriage, Tolstoy's battlefield, Stendhal's provinces. In his scene and in Stendhal, act and language are sharply divergent, even contradictory. Talk has little to do with perceived or experienced fact. Here as in Stendhal the hands seek each other, meet, have real sensate being: Romero has a smooth skin, fine hand, and small wrist that Brett reaches out for "as she spread the fingers apart." But the language—about bulls, and telling fortunes, and living long—has nothing to do with the subject. The real script is not visible. Talk and gesture need to be—as this dialogue will eventually put it—"understood."

Brett says to Jake that Romero has a good hand and will live a long time. That is not what is on her mind. Romero understands, forcing her to "Say it to me. Not to your friend." It is the repetition and not the statement that matters. Meaning is not denotation. One of the central problems of the ending is developed when language is addressed:

> "You know English well."
> "Yes," he said. "Pretty well, sometimes. But I must not let anybody know. It would be very bad, a torero who speaks English."
> "Why?" asked Brett.
> "It would be bad. The people would not like it. Not yet."
> "Why not?"
> "They would not like it. Bull-fighters are not like that."
> "What are bull-fighters like?"

Quantities have little connection to definition: "English" means a Protestant woman who has been in too many beds. "What are bull-fighters like?" means that Romero may be measured against them. When Romero adds that he must "forget English," the implication has nothing to do with language: he is telling her that she may be more trouble than she is sexually worth. And when that part of the dialogue is capped—

> "Don't forget it, yet," Brett said.
> "No?"
> "No."
> "All right."

—she has assured him that she will be worth his education. The change from question mark to period means something. Repetition and emphasis matter greatly: "No" twice stated means "Yes."

Brett says that she would like to have a hat like the one he is wearing and means that she would like to have him; he answers that he will get her one, which is self-evident. She is assertive—"Right. See that you do."—in a way that upsets his authority. Her own meaning is that a sexual agreement has been reached, although he may not be familiar with it. Jake understands all this, choosing that moment in which to leave. The rest of the dialogue is dense, and needs to be seen whole:

> I stood up. Romero rose, too.
> "Sit down," I said. "I must go and find our friends and bring them here." He looked at me. It was a final look to ask if it were understood. It was understood all right.
> "Sit down," Brett said to him. "You must teach me Spanish."
> He sat down and looked at her across the table. I went out. The hard-eyed people at the bull-fighter table watched me go. It was not pleasant. When I came back and looked in the cafe, twenty minutes later, Brett and Pedro Romero were gone. The coffee-glasses and our three empty cognac-glasses were on the table. A waiter came with a cloth and picked up the glasses and mopped off the table.

There is studied courtesy, ironic on the part of both men: diplomacy is the right mode for understanding fictions posing as truths. Jake takes the lead because he is the most experienced in this line of work. The ease with which Brett gets him to help her shows that he knows the drill. Nevertheless, it costs something for him to tell Romero to sit back down: there are three detectable lies in one sentence and a number of polite fictions. He does not have to go; if he does go he will certainly not look for his friends; and if he finds them he will not be bringing them here. Among the inferences: that friends are real friends, and that the whole procedure has some kind of clarity. But Rinaldi, understanding Frederic Henry in a dozen words, really does have it right the first time: the scene began with Brett saying that "I've never felt such a bitch" . . . "I do feel such a bitch" . . . "Oh, I do feel such a bitch."

Language does not suffice, which is why Romero "looked at me." There may not be a way in which actually to state a particular thought: "It was a final look to ask if it were understood. It was understood all right." It's not that Romero knows anything about either Wittgenstein or encoded dialogue, but he is aware that some things become less accurate through statement. The idea goes against the grain, but the double use of "understood" does more than remind us of the distance of language from fact; it characterizes the theater of social relationship. Rather a lot could be written about Jake's five-word phrase. He understands that what happens is probably one event in a sequence, that it will cost him more than assent, and that this is what happens when you take a stand on a slippery slope.

Brett's telling Romero to teach her Spanish has about as much to do with language as his saying that he knows limited English. *Corto y derecho,* it means what we think it does. It is unpleasant leaving the table only if one presumes that all the alternative meanings I have provided are the real meanings, and all the stated meanings don't matter very much. What has gone on is transparent to witnesses, and something has happened to Jake as well as to Brett and Romero. Jake returns twenty minutes later, without having seen his friends, and knowing that he will find an empty table. There is no reason for that to have happened except for pointing out the contradictions of the dialogue. It turns out, then, that to make things "understood" has very little denotative value. We "understand" the difference between statement and fact. Is that far-fetched? Within a few pages Hemingway caps this scene with another, which imposes a translation, and, finally, tells us what we have read:

> "Oh, go to hell, Cohn," Mike called from the table. "Brett's gone off with the bull-fighter chap. They're on their honeymoon."
> "You shut up."
> "Oh, go to hell!" Mike said languidly.
> "Is that where she is?" Cohn turned to me.
> "Go to hell!"
> "She was with you. Is that where she is?"
> "Go to hell!"
> "I'll make you tell me"—he stepped forward—"you damned pimp." (190)

6

Hemingway's Limits

Hemingway's "A Clean, Well-Lighted Place" appeared in *Scribner's Magazine* in March 1933. His letters in the year before its publication have much to say about writers and writing. One letter informs Paul Romaine that he is aware of the current "Leftward Swing" of American writers but does not himself "follow the fashions in politics, letters, religion etc." He is unlike Dreiser, Edmund Wilson, and John Dos Passos because "there is no left and right in writing. There is only good and bad writing." Another letter of 1932, this one to Dos Passos himself, raises an important philosophical point, stating that all systems eventually fail, including both Communism and what he calls the "management" of Christianity. Yet another sardonically suggests the advantages of anarchy. He urges Dos Passos to concentrate in his next novel not on abstract ideas but on the real characterological work of literature: "Keep them people, people, people, and don't let them get to be symbols."[1] That may have been a warning to himself, applicable to a story in which person and symbol are hard to separate. And, in which there is little left to believe.

The kinds of language in "A Clean, Well-Lighted Place" may roughly be described as naturalistic and allusive. The former corresponds to some actuality—so far as it may be conceived—while the latter draws some kind of relationship. The former has dominated analysis of the story.[2] Dialogue is deceptively simple, but its questions generate answers with little authority. Certain terms imply double meanings and have dual being.[3] They move the story necessarily from the naturalistic to the allusive and allegorical. The story seems to limit itself to the literal meanings of its title, yet we know that the title's elements have special meanings for Hemingway. The text states that "the light is very good" (382) but we know that our soul can go out of us "if it were dark" (367).[4] Shadows are in the story, but night and shadow are also places of the mind. One subject, the idea of "nothing," has a vast intellectual history of its own, as does "despair." Even the most naturalistic quantities of the story have entirely other selves.

There is a warrant for that: Hemingway kept returning to medieval Catholic and seventeenth-century Anglo-Catholic writing for titles and allusive ideas.[5] That is by now common critical knowledge, but some specifics might be added: "God is delighted in cleanlines, both bodily and ghostly"; to be "decent" and "clean" and staid is to be Christian; to see that rooms are "kept cleane and handsome" is a figure of the good life; to be composed and silent and civil is in some measure to be independent of one's miseries; to show compassion for "others miseries" is also to show the capacity for intellectual and spiritual being.[6] The word "clean" in one of its incarnations means uncorrupted by the normal practices of the world.[7] The tradition from which this terminology comes is of course that of meditation on death—a principal subject of metaphysical poetry and of Hemingway's story. The tradition emphasizes sight, hearing, and the ability "to see with the eyes of the imagination."[8] Whether one can do so is an issue of the story.

The opening refers itself to the light and shadow that make up visual experience. We assume that visual disclosure, essential to realism, will here also provide meanings. There is much to draw from relentlessly objective description: the fact of the old man sitting in the shadow, the flash of implication when the girl and soldier cross the stage at curfew. Viewed in itself the opening is about phenomena; it is impacted with information about time and place, the circumstance of age, appearance, and motion ("the street light shone on the brass number on his collar") peripherally discerned. And yet, some kinds of writing demand our understanding that "objects of nature are turned into symbols," while landscape itself may be symbol.[9]

The pace of the opening seems uncontrived, yet references to the passage of time accumulate, and begin to imply alternate meanings. A sequence of chronology begins: there has been the attempt at suicide last week, the approaching curfew, the beginning of the night, the schedule of the guard, the time for sleep, the hour of three approaching, the end of life, the time to stop drinking, the reminder again that three o'clock approaches, the time to return to bed, the time for lying awake, and finally the appearance of daylight. More than one kind of urgency is conveyed. Paul Tillich has written of the multiple meanings in "real" time: "Meaning can be found in situations and configurations of nature. We refer to the old and also to the new belief that such complexes express something which can be 'read' out of them. . . . The power inherent in natural configurations is also visible in the rhythms of certain recurring events, like day and night, summer and winter, seedtime and harvest, and also in the rhythms of human life."[10] Some quantities don't belong exclusively either to nature or symbol. Time in literature necessarily has two identities, current and recurrent. The temporal breaks its own limits, and "configurations of nature" are understood to extend past accepted definitions. But there is another point: "A Clean, Well-Lighted Place" accumulates the meanings of time, lets us know the essential fact that more than one kind of time is impending. All of the small references add up to one very large reference: that the time has come to face death. For one of the protagonists, that is; for the others it is the time to face reality. All three protagonists understand these things and react in different ways. Even a joke about getting home early extends our sense of what is possible as against what is expected. Getting cut down from a rope in time may not be a solution.

Narration of the opening page is also stage direction.[11] The "terrace" outside the cafe is a well-defined area outside the building, apart from the trees and street. Movement occurs across stage, with the soldier and the girl in a hurry. They have walk-on roles—an entrance and an exit—but their brief, wordless advent is thematic. The scenery displays light against dark, enclosure against space, silence against movement, a single figure "in the shadow" isolated as the center of meaning. There is an audience on stage, which is a conventional mechanism for explaining the meaning, not otherwise easily managed, of a scene without dialogue. A rhythmic pattern of sounds begins; we hear commentary from the chorus, then noises of motion, then the distinctive hard rapping on the saucer that begins the action. So far, all is within the phenomenological world. But, a particular kind of dramatic structure is, I think, involved. We have seen it before, because it is an essential part of literary history, and we note that this scene may be a new production of an old original. The characters are unnamed, which suggests the kind of drama involved.[12]

Allegorical drama features a central figure along with opposed voices that speak to him and often for him. Its subject will be spiritual choice. There will always be a decision that must be made. The text will display correspondences between things said and seen and their extended meanings: it is late not because night comes but because there are overwhelming questions that arrive at certain times of life.[13] These questions need absolute clarification within limited time. *Limited time is life itself.* Time dominates, expressed not only by continual allusion to passing minutes and hours but through the growth of awareness.

It exceeds realism to have one unnamed character of Hemingway's story be young, a second middle-aged, and the third old. The sequence of ages approximately doubled corresponds more to Bacon's essay "Of Youth and Age" than to demographic probability.[14] The main characters are true to their own naturalistic lives while they imply also the life of *Everyman,* a drama in which this one has its roots. Typology has something to add to our understanding of the text—the young waiter is a version of youth described in many texts about "characters" or stages of life and occupation. A classic of this form, still shrewd, tells us that youth is necessarily "mingled with the vices of the age," an idea that Hemingway has transposed—and also that it "scornes and feares, and yet hopes for old age."[15] Those fears are useful to remember.[16]

We may see the scene first with unimpaired visual authority suggesting an objective and naturalistic world, but we come also to see it in more complex and allusive terms. Robert Herrick, who worked within the poetic so much admired by T. S. Eliot, called the following a "divination" of meaning:

When a Daffadil I see,
Hanging down his head t'wards me;
Guesse I may, what I must be:

> First, I shall decline my head;
> Secondly, I shall be dead;
> Lastly, safely buryed.[17]

There are correspondences of this sort that we detect in the mention of time, light, shadow, and especially that "despair" that exists ever so momentarily in this story, in small type in a small mind. Clearly, the older waiter detects many correspondences between himself and the old man as objects of nature. (One always looks for the presence of T. S. Eliot, especially when the triad of modernism, language, and literary history is involved. In discussing the roots of modernism, Alfred Alvarez finds this kind of thought to be essential and locates models for it. He cites at length an essay by Eliot in 1923 about the ways "in which we may find a poet to be modern." The essay is about the school of Donne, and it defines the contributions that school can make to writing in the twenties: providing a model of "complicated states of mind" nowhere else available.) Modern writing involves an act of recovery allowing us to find relationships between perceived things.[18]

The form this story takes strongly implies that things have more than one meaning but that, after all, there *is* a meaning. The form suggests that conflict between worldly and spiritual beliefs can and will be resolved. But the action taking place within the space provided by the formal structure is subject to a different kind of argument.

In "A Clean, Well-Lighted Place," most of the information we get about the three main characters comes from dialogue. There is necessarily a connection between dialogue and character, as H. E. Bates wrote when comparing Aldous Huxley and Hemingway. Bates concluded that the latter had in fact used ideas to create "living people."[19] But the former had used people simply to mouth ideas, which is one of the things that Hemingway's 1932 correspondence warned against. The Bates essay should be treated with respect, but it errs when claiming that Hemingway captures reality by reproducing the "instinctive, thoughtless language" of the models for his characters.[20] The premise is that those models can't think, hence the ordinariness of their ideas and the persuasiveness of Hemingway's prose recording them. A different premise makes more sense: those models are limited by language itself. And, they get their ideas from the same places we all do. Language described as "thoughtless" does not really apply to the dialogues of "A Clean, Well-Lighted Place" because the language is full of thought at least attempted. But even a philosopher might have a hard time making sense of the situation.

Before saying that the younger waiter and the older waiter in this story have limited minds or morals it might be more rigorous to say that they apply explanation to circumstance. That is the burden of the dialogue. Their explanation is not successful, although the closer it comes to being a summary of action the more reliable it seems to be. They labor under two kinds of limitations: their governing ideas, and the language they use to state them. One might say not that they state ideas but transmit them. The younger waiter is not original, he applies received opinions about money and happiness and masculinity to a case that might exemplify them. Those are external opinions, the residue of our culture's intention to order and interpret our lives, to give us a common language of explanation. He has no quarrel with ideas, a point made with great specificity when he thinks categorically: "You talk like an old man yourself." This is far more important than may appear because it crosses a philosophical dividing line between the self and what might be called its manufactured sources. The older waiter, more insightful, pursues ideas that come from reflections on the failure of culture to provide answers. In neither case are explanations helped by the language stating them.

We are often advised to see values in this story. But, one of Hemingway's warnings to writers in the early thirties establishes certain points: "Don't just think who is right. . . . As a writer you should not judge. You should understand."[21] For the present I argue only that the old man has the integrity of silence; the other two are betrayed into the inconsistencies of language.

There are certainly problems of character in this story, but they are implied by problems of statement. The very terms that the two waiters use are insufficient for this dialogue. In that, they are representative of their time. For example, Whitehead wrote in the mid-twenties that he had little confidence in our power to identify or even to discuss human concerns. He suggested that poetic logic might be an improvement on scientific logic, that "Wordsworth, to the height of genius, expresses the concrete facts of our apprehension, facts which are distorted in the scientific analysis. Is it not possible that the standardised concepts of science are only valid within narrow limitations?"[22] Whitehead shared with James, Dewey, and certainly with Hemingway the view that "the concrete facts of our apprehension" were by no means easily interpreted. A second point: "Though there is a common world of thought associated with our sense-perceptions, there is no common world to think about. What we do think about is a common conceptual world applying indifferently to our individual experiences which are strictly personal to ourselves."[23] That idea is especially worth recalling in regard to Hemingway. When he refers to "people" in his letters or creates them here he necessarily refers to an *idea* about people. What exactly is that concept in this story?

The two waiters have a difficult time understanding the old man, and also framing questions and finding answers that make sense. The language available to them is too crude to get at the issues raised by the circumstances. That may be true for those outside the story. Harry Levin's "Observations on the Style of Ernest Hemingway" makes the point that language in general depreciates. English has by no means been kept up by the culture around us, a culture to which we are now very nearly normatively opposed. Ideas are cheap and language is commercial. To see the way language is used is to suspect where it comes from. It is not as if a whole linguistic world of material precision and moral sensibility lay open before the younger waiter and the older waiter could they only bring themselves to address it:

> It is not Hemingway, but the sloganmongers of our epoch, who have debased the language; he has been attempting to restore some decent degree of correspondence between words and things; and the task of verification is a heavy one, which throws the individual back on his personal resources of awareness. That he has succeeded within limits, and with considerable strain, is less important than that he has succeeded, that a few more aspects of life have been captured for literature. Meanwhile the

word continues to dematerialize, and has to be made flesh all over again.[24]

This needs its context: the heavy task of reform was often addressed in the twenties. Eliot was particularly important because he connected the reform of language to the recovery of seventeenth-century models of prose and poetry, models that affect this story. He argued in 1926 that "we have a vocabulary for everything and exact ideas about nothing," and that "a word half-understood, torn from its place in some alien or half-formed science, as of psychology, conceals from both writer and reader the meaninglessness of a statement." His standard was that of Lancelot Andrewes, a writer who kept "squeezing and squeezing the word until it yields a full juice of meaning which we should never have supposed any word to possess."[25] This meant as much for Eliot's conception of writing in the twenties as it did for his rediscovery of the Jacobeans. Hemingway, often allusive in his own work, reversed the equation, writing instead about words with all meaning drained out of them. One insistent tactic is the introduction of writers such as Horatio Alger or W. H. Hudson or H. G. Wells to suggest triviality of thought, another is the use of traceable "ideas" in circulation.

The depreciation of language was one of the subjects of public philosophy. Shortly before Eliot began to write about meaningless statement, John Dewey had attacked "words . . . easily taken for ideas." The modern failure at comprehension of human relationships—he called it a "deluge of half-observations, of verbal ideas, and unassimilated 'knowledge' which afflicts the world"—was in his view characteristic of the twenties. Dewey was especially concerned with the simulation of thought, i.e., the practice of citing "catchwords" and "verbal formula" that allowed us to forego two things: the perception of reality and, equally important, any true "discernment of relationships."[26] This was the mainstream of philosophical thought, not the periphery of literary criticism. In order to think with any accuracy about perceiving sensory or intellectual realities, novelists like Hemingway needed to think in line with Dewey, and also Whitehead, Russell, and Wittgenstein.

One issue of this story is that outmoded ideas do not explain human behavior; a second issue is that current certainties also fail to explain it. The mode is recurrent statement followed by explanation. But what confidence is it possible to have in the norms of that relationship? According to Wittgenstein, who set the ground rules for understanding language in the twenties, what we ordinarily see as communication may be something entirely different: language "sets everyone the same traps; it is an immense network of easily accessible wrong turnings." Like Whitehead, he saw those "concrete facts" of apprehension as subjective, closed off, not available to other minds, or, indeed, to our own. Here is Wittgenstein in 1930 on a problem of statement exemplified by the "Nada" part of Hemingway's text: "Each of the sentences I write is trying to say . . . the same thing over and over again; it is as though they were all simply views of one object seen from different angles." Thoughts may not progress at all, but become a kind of "infinite regress."[27] Under the penumbra of these ideas of limitation the problems of "A Clean, Well-Lighted Place" inherently resist clarification. The answer to that oft-cited comic turn, "Can we talk?" is, of course, no.

The first dialogue has its own critical history.[28] I won't assign lines to speakers when the text is unclear, but will follow broadly the conclusions of Warren Bennett, who states that "it is the older waiter, the character voice of the author, who recognizes the impossibility of 'knowing,' and particularly, the impossibility of knowing the psychological complexity of another person":[29]

> "Last week he tried to commit suicide," one waiter said.
> "Why?"
> "He was in despair."
> "What about?"
> "Nothing."
> "How do you know it was nothing?"
> "He has plenty of money." (379)

This burst of speech is short, accurate, and deceptively simple. The ideas are not simple. In order to get from the first question to the last answer no matter who is credited with dialogue, a part of the intellectual history of the West needs to be traversed. Isaiah Berlin writes of our recurring assumption—it is a kind of curse of philosophy—that all questions are questions of fact. We want to believe that there is "a solution for every problem" and that finding it is only a matter of means.[30] As Berlin sees it, the conviction that answers for things human are "discoverable in principle" is plainly wrong. The Hemingway letters that I have cited make the same point, so that it is unsurprising for the younger waiter to be a kind of trolley-stop for false marketplace explanations of our lives. His ideas have come from some source to reach him, and it is reasonably clear that the source is worldly reason (exactly as in allegory) convinced of its own realism. Because it is free of illusions, it allows itself to believe that it is free of errors. But, the point made by Hemingway about systems does not exempt anything.

Literary history is layered in this story. *Everyman* confronts despair with the argument that "money maketh all right that is wrong." *The Pilgrim's Progress* redefines argument itself: the character named Young Ignorance insistently invokes reason. Relying on "the natural apprehensions of all flesh" he brings rationality to a place in which it cannot work and he is dismissive of what he calls the "distracted brains" and "whimsies" that read more into things than he can accept.[31] The voice I take to be that of the young waiter concludes that everything can be reduced to something else. But we know that quantities like "despair" or "nothing" are finally uncontainable. The demotion of "despair" to lowercase print is as relevant as finding it to be dependent on money. As for that most complex word in Hemingway, "Why?" it makes sequential appearances, each of which refers itself to others:

> "Why did he kill himself, Daddy?"
> "I don't know, Nick. He couldn't stand things, I guess." (95)

The point of Hemingway's questions—this is from one of his earliest works, "Indian Camp"—is that there are no answers. Language is itself an obstacle to their understanding.

Individuals duplicate the instructions of culture, a point made by the next major burst of dialogue. Speech rhythms of statement and response that normally follow upon each other are broken up first by the old man demanding more brandy, then by the younger waiter shifting intellectual gears as he begins to think of his own life. The change from one subject to another in this story is characteristic.

> The old man looked at him. "Another brandy," he said.
> "You'll be drunk," the waiter said. The old man looked at him. The waiter went away.
> "He'll stay all night," he said to his colleague. "I'm sleepy now. I never get into bed before three o'clock. He should have killed himself last week." (380)

One wants to notice the relationship, or rather its absence, between "Another brandy" and "He should have killed himself last week." The incomprehensible distance between the two statements adds another layer of questioning to a story already defined by questions. Because the questions asked by the text provoke answers so badly connected to them it becomes necessary to provide different answers; that is how we know that the answers stated by the text are wrong.

Is the younger waiter's explanation a moral issue? It exists in the privileged space within which one considers one's own demands as reality itself. There is a shock of recognition because we prefer not to admit that one statement can draw forth such another, but we do know that it can. The distance between the two statements is very great, but it is also very short when measured by the demands of the self. When we recognize that, we recognize also the degree to which historical time has intruded itself. One now needs no apology to be absolutely self-referential, not even ironic demurrer.

There is a connection between "What did he want to kill himself for?" and "How much money has he got?" The second question necessarily modifies the first:

> "He's drunk now," he said.
> "He's drunk every night."
> "What did he want to kill himself for?"
> "How should I know."
> "How did he do it?"

"He hung himself with a rope."
"Who cut him down?"
"His niece."
"Why did they do it?"
"Fear for his soul."
"How much money has he got?"
"He's got plenty." (380)

The passage cited has been looked over by many critics, and one is grateful for the combination of "naturalistic" and "symbolic" explanation, the attempt to weave together the meaning of statement and of moral problems that it expresses.[32] But there are issues other than the opposition between old and young, or between compassion and indifference, and I think that those other issues are more important. The passage restates three discontinuous ideas: it would be good to know the reason why, it is not possible to know the reason why, and understanding the reason why is only a matter of means. The two participants in the dialogue keep bumping against the limits of knowing, as if their dialogue had been written by Wittgenstein. One of them is convinced that there are answers to his questions, but he has become, intellectually, the low man on the totem pole.

Some phrases used in the dialogue have especially refractive power. One of these, "soul," should be measured against its recent use in a dialogue between Frederic Henry and Count Greffi toward the end of *A Farewell to Arms*:

"I don't know about the soul."
"Poor boy. We none of us know about the soul."[33]

The weight of this conclusion affects any interpretation of the "soul" in "A Clean, Well-Lighted Place." The second phrase I have in mind is "confidence," something with more than psychological implications. Much is made of this term. We ought to recognize the sources of that confidence. Opinion comes from the wreckage of ideas, from glib generalizations of the marketplace. The younger waiter is confident because he can impose explanations that he assumes are unarguable: money causes happiness, wives are where husbands think they are, the old are in a separate category, and the demands of the self are the understood locus for the development of any argument. The two phrases about the knowable and its opposite are necessarily in conflict, and no single standard can be applied to them.

We do not imagine that the younger waiter reads Wittgenstein, but we do know that he lives in a world that Wittgenstein defined.[34] It is important to note that Wittgenstein developed two ideas: the first of them being that "if a question can be put at all, then it *can* also be answered"; the second that "even if *all possible* scientific questions be answered, the problems of life have still not been touched at all."[35] The first of these allows the reader to expect a functional answer when he encounters one that isn't. The second reminds us (even Bertrand Russell was forced to agree) that some things are mysteries.[36] To a certain extent, there is indeed a "meaning" to these lines, or there should be a meaning, or, within limits, could be a meaning. But, is there a meaning? Or, better put, is there a meaning available at this particular time in 1932?

Is the problem that the young waiter is mean-spirited and the old waiter uncertain? Or is it that meanings differ? Both formulations may be true, but the latter seems more likely. Interpretations present themselves according to unmerciful logic. We will, I think, never be able to understand the silence of the old man drinking brandy; we can make some attempt to contextualize it; we can't explain it through ourselves, or vice versa. The story's central problem does not represent what is now tediously called a problem of communication. Communication itself is the problem. If the younger waiter were ten times more compassionate, he still would be unable to understand the situation.[37] First, he is subject to philosophical limits. Second, he is subject to this particular historical moment, and at this moment character is in a special way self-referential. If the idea is to create convincing "people," then this man is representative of some theory about them. The issue is only indirectly connected to ethics and empathy. Something has become true in modern life that limits understanding. It almost certainly resides in the power of communicated ideas. One of the most interesting things in the text is the shabbiness of the younger waiter's ideas. They are clearly wrong but easy to believe because they are in circulation.

In the last dialogue, the younger waiter is insistently subjective. Hemingway's technique is to organize his remarks around pronouns: "I want to go home to bed. . . . You talk like an old man yourself. . . . Are you trying to insult me? . . . I am all confidence" (381–82). It would appear that he has a strong sense of his own mind. But, the "I" of this set of statements is, I think, artificial, a character only momentarily endowed with a sense of self. The younger waiter's individuation does not come from confidence in himself. He has a *reflexive* sense of identity, hence of reality.[38] We can tell that because that confidence is so quickly shaken, and because there is finally only a single set of motives that are clear to him. Hemingway uses a different strategy for the older waiter who is, so to speak, subjectively invisible, temporally dislocated. He invokes things outside himself: "What is an hour? . . . An hour is the same . . . also, now, there are shadows of the leaves" (381–82). His arguments develop from outside the self and have their origin precisely in the lack of confidence in culturally transmitted truisms.

There is another measure of self, involving that persistent term "confidence" that is, I think, as much a *reference* as a characteristic. The younger waiter has few doubts about the standards that he invokes, accepting and then putting to work derived conceptions. Part of his "confidence" derives from knowing that they are available and assuming that they are right. There are several reasons for the reader's lack of confidence in his ideas. As to the first, we know that we are rarely masters of our own "fields of actual experience."[39] To experience is by no means to know, to state is by no means to explain. As to the second, there is so great a residue of materialism and conformity in the younger waiter's references that we instinctively deny their legitimacy. The opening images of curfew and military police should be on our minds because they are parabolic. They extend to the ideas that he plucks out of the atmosphere, and to the sense of self, so plainly manufactured, to which he appeals. He imagines a public of many like himself, all in agreement.

"A Clean, Well-Lighted Place" gains depth by its allusions to a more spiritually generous literature of the past. That literature once had the power to state and perhaps even to resolve our dilemmas. But it is gone, along with its culture, and this story takes place in our time. The values of the younger waiter are recognizably those of our material world, while those of the older waiter seem to be admirable relics of a lost past. Nearly everything we get to know in this story is surmise: facts (if they may be said to exist) transmitted in a form, conversational dialogue, inherently subject to error. The text is composed not of sequential logical developments of ideas but of language disengaged from meanings. If character is made up of anything, it is made up of language, and the fundamental disconnection of language, idea, and fact is the text's central point.

NOTES

Introduction

1. See Gillian Beer, "Wave Theory and the Rise of Literary Modernism," in *Open Fields: Science in Cultural Encounter* (Oxford: Oxford University Press, 1999), 295–318.

2. F. Scott Fitzgerald, *F. Scott Fitzgerald: A Life in Letters,* ed. Matthew J. Bruccoli with Judith S. Baughman (New York: Touchstone, 1995); F. Scott Fitzgerald, *F. Scott Fitzgerald on Authorship,* ed. Matthew J. Bruccoli with Judith S. Baughman (Columbia: University of South Carolina Press, 1996); Robert F. Moss, "An American Man of Letters," in Thomas Cooper Library, *F. Scott Fitzgerald: Centenary Exhibition* (Columbia: University of South Carolina Press, 1996), 59–60.

3. Fitzgerald, *F. Scott Fitzgerald: A Life in Letters,* 162–64.

4. See Walter Lippmann, *Drift and Mastery: An Attempt to Diagnose the Current Unrest* (New York: Mitchell Kennerley, 1914), 174–75.

5. Fitzgerald, *F. Scott Fitzgerald: A Life in Letters,* 164–67.

6. F. Scott Fitzgerald, *The Great Gatsby,* ed. Matthew J. Bruccoli (Cambridge: Cambridge University Press, 1991), 107.

7. Sinclair Lewis, *Babbitt* (1922; reprint, New York: Signet, 1980), 150.

8. United States, President's Research Committee on Social Trends, *Recent Social Trends in the United States: Report of the President's Research Committee on Social Trends,* 2 vols. (New York: McGraw-Hill, 1933), 2: 979–80.

9. Alfred North Whitehead, "Science and the Modern World," in *Alfred North Whitehead: An Anthology,* ed. F. S. C. Northrop and Mason W. Gross (New York: Macmillan, 1953), 438–40.

10. Whitehead, "Symbolism, Its Meaning and Effect," in *Alfred North Whitehead,* 540–43.

11. George Santayana, *The Sense of Beauty* (1896; reprint, New York: Dover, 1955), 46.

12. Walter Lippmann, "Upton Sinclair," in *Public Persons* (New York: Liveright, 1976), 33–34. The essay appeared in 1911.

13. John Dewey, *The Philosophy of John Dewey*, ed. John J. McDermott (Chicago: University of Chicago Press, 1981), 642–43.

14. Dewey, "Existence, Value, and Criticism," in *Philosophy of John Dewey*, 335.

15. Dewey, "Experience and Philosophic Method," in *Philosophy of John Dewey*, 257.

16. Lionel Trilling, "Hemingway and His Critics," in *Speaking of Literature and Society* (New York: Harcourt Brace Jovanovich, 1980), 125.

17. Lippmann, "Upton Sinclair," in *Public Persons*, 33.

18. Lionel Trilling, "F. Scott Fitzgerald," in *The Liberal Imagination* (New York: Viking Press, 1950), 247–49.

19. Santayana, *Sense of Beauty*, 104. Russell's statement is in his Introduction to Ludwig Wittgenstein's *Tractatus Logico-Philosophicus* (1922; reprint, Mineola, N.Y.: Dover, 1999), 8.

Chapter 1

1. Isaiah Berlin, *The Roots of Romanticism,* ed. Henry Hardy (Princeton: Princeton University Press, 1999), 16–18. A. O. Lovejoy, "On the Discrimination of Romanticisms," in *Essays in the History of Ideas* (Baltimore: Johns Hopkins University Press, 1948), 228–53. See the important essay on romantic meanings by Iain McCalman in his Introduction to his edition of *An Oxford Companion to the Romantic Age: British Culture 1776–1832* (Oxford: Oxford University Press, 2001), 1–11.

2. Ruth Prigozy, "Fitzgerald, Paris, and the Romantic Imagination," in *French Connections,* ed. J. Gerald Kennedy and Jackson R. Bryer (New York: St. Martin's Press, 1999), 161–71. See also Richard Lehan, "The Romantic Self and the Uses of Place in the Stories of F. Scott Fitzgerald," in *The Short Stories of F. Scott Fitzgerald: New Approaches in Criticism,* ed. Jackson R. Bryer (Madison: University of Wisconsin Press, 1982), 3–21.

3. See Thomas A. Boyd's interview, "Literary Libels—Francis Scott Key Fitzgerald," in F. Scott Fitzgerald, *F. Scott Fitzgerald on Authorship,* ed. Matthew J. Bruccoli with Judith S. Baughman (Columbia: University of South Carolina Press, 1996), 64. I have relied on this book, which is the best collection of Fitzgerald's literary opinions.

4. Fitzgerald's use of the term "romantic" contains a number of meanings. Romanticism came to him from two sources: direct reading of Wordsworth, Keats, and early-nineteenth-century British writers, and the diffusion of their ideas by Emerson, Whitman, and American Victorians. The British romantics had a tempered view of potentiality: Milton R. Stern has reminded me that they "conceded" to historical necessity. American romantics were less willing to limit vision by the facts or implications of historical experience. We need to be aware of both kinds of thought. Additionally, although Fitzgerald used the term "romantic" to describe the importance of certain moments in

life, he also used it to describe emotional triviality. Romantic feeling had become, he knew, a form of sentimentality in novels, films, and the love story so much in demand in magazines of the twenties.

5. See H. L. Mencken's account of poetry as "an escape from life" in "The Poet and His Art," in *A Mencken Chrestomathy* (New York: Alfred A. Knopf, 1967), 449–58. Originally published in the *Smart Set,* June 1920.

6. William James, *William James: Writings 1902–1910,* ed. Bruce Kuklick (New York: Literary Classics of the United States, 1987), 606–8.

7. Van Wyck Brooks, "Letters and Leadership," in *America's Coming-of-Age* (Garden City, N.Y.: Doubleday, 1958), 141–43. Originally published in *Letters and Leadership,* 1918. See his survey of "The Literary Life" as the twenties began in Harold E. Stearns, ed., *Civilization in the United States* (London: Jonathan Cape, 1922), 179–97. In the same volume see also Conrad Aiken's survey of the kinds of poetry being written, 215–26.

8. Stephen L. Tanner, *Paul Elmer More: Literary Criticism as the History of Ideas* (Albany: State University of New York Press, 1987), 51–57.

9. Irving Babbitt, *Rousseau and Romanticism* (Boston: Houghton Mifflin, 1919), 353–93.

10. Mark Girouard, *The Return to Camelot: Chivalry and the English Gentleman* (New Haven: Yale University Press, 1981), 249–93.

11. See Paul Fussell, *The Great War and Modern Memory* (New York: Oxford University Press, 1975), 21–23.

12. See Ludwig Wittgenstein, *Tractatus Logico-Philosophicus* (1922; reprint, Mineola, N.Y.: Dover, 1999), 103–8, and Bertrand Russell's Introduction, 8–11; John Dewey, "Search for the Great Community," in *The Later Works, 1925–1953,* 2 vols., ed. Jo Ann Boydston (Carbondale: Southern Illinois University Press, 1981), 2: 341.

13. Geoffrey H. Hartman, "Romanticism and Antiself-Consciousness," in *Romanticism: Points of View,* ed. Robert F. Gleckner and Gerald E. Enscoe (Englewood Cliffs, N.J.: Prentice-Hall, 1970), 295.

14. Edmund Wilson, "The Anarchists of Taste: Who First Broke the Rules of Harmony in the Modern World," in *From the Uncollected Edmund Wilson,* ed. Janet Groth and David Castronovo (Athens: Ohio University Press, 1995), 76.

15. "Prediction Is Made about James Joyce Novel: F. S. Fitzgerald Believes *Ulysses* Is Great Book of Future," unsigned article in *Richmond Times-Dispatch,* 24 June 1923, Sec. 2, p. 5, in Fitzgerald, *F. Scott Fitzgerald on Authorship,* 91.

16. See Ronald Berman, *The Great Gatsby and Modern Times* (Urbana: University of Illinois Press, 1996), 17.

17. Fitzgerald, "Sherwood Anderson on the Marriage Question," in *F. Scott Fitzgerald on Authorship,* 84.

18. Fitzgerald, "Public Letter to Thomas Boyd," in *F. Scott Fitzgerald on Authorship,* 43.

19. Fitzgerald, "Three Soldiers," in *F. Scott Fitzgerald on Authorship*, 48.

20. Earl Wasserman, "The English Romantics: The Grounds of Knowledge," in *Romanticism: Points of View*, 335.

21. Ibid., 346.

22. Fitzgerald, "Minnesota's Capital in the Role of Main Street," in *F. Scott Fitzgerald on Authorship*, 82.

23. See Berman, *The Great Gatsby and Modern Times*, 15–37.

24. Fitzgerald, "Three Cities," in *F. Scott Fitzgerald on Authorship*, 51–52.

25. See Ronald Berman, *The Great Gatsby and Fitzgerald's World of Ideas* (Tuscaloosa: University of Alabama Press, 1997), 175–200.

26. F. Scott Fitzgerald, *The Crack-Up*, ed. Edmund Wilson (New York: New Directions, 1945), 81. See John F. Callahan, *The Illusions of a Nation: Myth and History in the Novels of F. Scott Fitzgerald* (Urbana: University of Illinois Press, 1972), 25–26.

27. Hoxie Neale Fairchild, *The Romantic Quest* (New York: Columbia University Press, 1931), 192–200.

28. Marilyn Butler, "Plotting the Revolution: The Political Narratives of Romantic Poetry and Criticism," in *Romantic Revolutions*, ed. Kenneth R. Johnston, Gilbert Chaitin, Karen Hanson, and Herbert Marks (Bloomington: Indiana University Press, 1990), 155. See Bruce L. Grenberg, "Fitzgerald's 'Crack-up' Essays Revisited: Fictions of the Self, Mirrors for a Nation," in *F. Scott Fitzgerald: New Perspectives*, ed. Jackson R. Bryer, Alan Margolies, and Ruth Prigozy (Athens: University of Georgia Press, 2000), 207: "Throughout the essays Fitzgerald makes a number of specific identifications between his own crack-up and the crisis experienced by the nation in the crash of 1929 and the economic-social depression that followed. . . . He explicitly identifies his personal history with the history of the nation."

29. Fitzgerald, "To: Robert D. Clark," in *F. Scott Fitzgerald on Authorship*, 41.

30. Berlin, *Roots of Romanticism*, 82.

31. Fitzgerald, "Poor Old Marriage," in *F. Scott Fitzgerald on Authorship*, 53.

32. Fitzgerald, "Aldous Huxley's *Crome Yellow*," in *F. Scott Fitzgerald on Authorship*, 59.

33. Fitzgerald, "Homage to the Victorians," in *F. Scott Fitzgerald on Authorship*, 73–74, 76.

34. Fitzgerald, *Crack-Up*, 89–90.

35. H. L. Mencken, "Civilization," in *The Philosophy of Friedrich Nietzsche* (Boston: Luce and Company, 1913), 164–71.

36. Fitzgerald, "Sherwood Anderson on the Marriage Question," in *F. Scott Fitzgerald on Authorship*, 83.

37. Mencken, *Philosophy of Friedrich Nietzsche*, 88–93.

38. Ibid., 160–67. See the discussion of Tom Buchanan's "ideas" about men, women, and social order in Berman, *The Great Gatsby and Fitzgerald's World of Ideas*, 150–51.

39. Fitzgerald, "Public Letter to Thomas Boyd," in *F. Scott Fitzgerald on Authorship,* 88.

40. M. H. Abrams, *Natural Supernaturalism* (New York: W. W. Norton, 1971), 379.

41. Ibid., 387.

42. Abrams, *Natural Supernaturalism,* 378; F. Scott Fitzgerald, "Under Fire," in *F. Scott Fitzgerald on Authorship,* 88.

43. Fitzgerald, "Under Fire," in *F. Scott Fitzgerald on Authorship,* 89.

44. Fairchild, *Romantic Quest,* 190.

45. Abrams, *Natural Supernaturalism,* 185, 190–91. See also Hartman, "Romanticism and Antiself-Consciousness," in *Romanticism: Points of View,* 288–89.

46. F. Scott Fitzgerald, *The Short Stories of F. Scott Fitzgerald,* ed. Matthew J. Bruccoli (New York: Charles Scribner's Sons, 1989), 235–36.

47. F. Scott Fitzgerald, *The Great Gatsby,* ed. Matthew J. Bruccoli (Cambridge: Cambridge University Press, 1991), 86.

48. Milton R. Stern, *The Golden Moment* (Urbana: University of Illinois Press, 1971), 253.

49. For discussion of the Fitzgerald passages cited see Robert Emmet Long, *The Achieving of The Great Gatsby* (Lewisburg, Pa.: Bucknell University Press, 1979), 96–98. There is a problem here common to much Fitzgerald criticism, which is to invoke the term "romantic" while failing to specify theories of romanticism.

50. Berlin, *Roots of Romanticism,* 134–39.

51. Lionel Trilling, "F. Scott Fitzgerald," in *F. Scott Fitzgerald: A Collection of Critical Essays,* ed. Arthur Mizener (Englewood Cliffs, N.J.: Prentice-Hall, 1963), 16.

52. René Wellek, "The Concept of Romanticism in Literary History," in *Romanticism: Points of View,* 205.

53. Fitzgerald, "How to Waste Material," in *F. Scott Fitzgerald on Authorship,* 105. See also 115: "F. Scott Fitzgerald Is Bored by Efforts at Realism in 'Lit.'"

CHAPTER 2

1. Charles A. Beard and Mary R. Beard, *The Rise of American Civilization,* 2 vols. (New York: Macmillan, 1927), 2: 800.

2. See for example R. G. Collingwood, *The Idea of Nature* (Oxford: Oxford University Press, 1945), and *The Idea of History* (Oxford: Oxford University Press, 1946); A. O. Lovejoy, "On the Discrimination of Romanticisms," in *Essays in the History of Ideas* (Baltimore: Johns Hopkins University Press, 1948), 228–53.

3. Sigmund Freud, *Civilization and Its Discontents,* ed. James Strachey (New York: W. W. Norton, 1961), 36.

4. Hendrik Willem Van Loon, "The American Naissance," *Vanity Fair* 18, no. 3 (May 1922): 41; see my discussion of Van Loon and others in *The Great Gatsby and Modern Times* (Urbana: University of Illinois Press, 1994), 20–33.

5. F. Scott Fitzgerald, *The Great Gatsby*, ed. Matthew J. Bruccoli (Cambridge: Cambridge University Press, 1991), 14.

6. See Walter Lippmann, *Public Opinion* (1922; reprint, New York: Free Press, 1997), 91. Lippmann cites Simon Strunsky's review of H. G. Wells's *Outline of History*.

7. Walter Lippmann, *Drift and Mastery* (New York: Mitchell Kennerley, 1914), 177.

8. To Stanley Dell, January 21, 1921, in Edmund Wilson, *Letters on Literature and Politics, 1912–1972*, ed. Elena Wilson (New York: Farrar, Straus and Giroux, 1977), 54.

9. George Santayana, *Character and Opinion in the United States* (Garden City, N.Y.: Doubleday Anchor, 1956), vi, 118–44.

10. See Fred Hobson, *Serpent in Eden: H. L. Mencken and the South* (Baton Rouge: Louisiana State University Press, 1974), 81.

11. See H. L. Mencken, *My Life as Author and Editor* (New York: Vintage, 1995), 259: "Fitz was himself no mean critic, and he saw clearly the hollowness of such notables of the time as Floyd Dell and Ernest Poole. Now and then he wrote book reviews, and when my *Prejudices: Second Series* appeared at the end of 1920 he reviewed it for the *Bookman*."

12. In Stearns, *Civilization in the United States*, 185, 196.

13. See Richard Lehan, *The Great Gatsby: The Limits of Wonder* (Boston: Twayne, 1990), 80–90.

14. To John Peale Bishop, September 6, 1923, in *Letters on Literature and Politics*, 111.

15. See Ronald Berman, *Fitzgerald, Hemingway, and the Twenties* (Tuscaloosa: University of Alabama Press, 2001), 15–18.

16. See Berman, *The Great Gatsby and Modern Times*, 24–25.

17. Ibid., 25–26.

18. See Berman, *Fitzgerald, Hemingway, and the Twenties*, 108.

19. Freud, *Civilization and Its Discontents*, 34.

20. H. Rider Haggard, *Allen Quatermain* (Oxford: Oxford University Press, 1995), 10–12. The novel was first published in 1887.

21. See Ezra Pound, "E. P. Ode Pour L'Election De Son Sepulchre," in *Personae* (New York: New Directions, 1971), 191.

22. See Paul Fussell, *The Great War and Modern Memory* (New York: Oxford University Press, 1975); Samuel Hynes, *A War Imagined* (New York: Atheneum, 1991); Modris Eksteins, *Rites of Spring* (Boston: Houghton Mifflin, 2000).

23. Edmund Wilson, *I Thought of Daisy* (1929; reprint, Harmondsworth, U.K.: Penguin Books, 1963), 217.

24. Ludwig Wittgenstein's Preface to *Philosophical Remarks* is reprinted in Hans-Johann Glock, "Wittgenstein and Reason," in *Wittgenstein: Biography and Philosophy*, ed. James C. Klagge (Cambridge: Cambridge University Press, 2001), 210–11.

25. Harry Salpeter, "Fitzgerald, Spenglerian," in *F. Scott Fitzgerald on Authorship*, ed. Matthew J. Bruccoli with Judith S. Baughman (Columbia: University of South Carolina Press, 1996), 111.

NOTES

26. F. Scott Fitzgerald, "Three Cities," in *F. Scott Fitzgerald on Authorship*, 51–52.

27. Stearns, *Civilization in the United States*, vii.

28. Harold E. Stearns, *Confessions of a Harvard Man*, ed. Hugh Ford (Sutton West, Ont., and Santa Barbara, Calif.: Paget Press, 1984), 69–75.

29. George Santayana, "Patriotism," in *The Life of Reason* (New York: Charles Scribner's Sons, 1919), 165. See Santayana's discussion in "Democracy" of a subject important to Fitzgerald's imagination, the relativity of civilization, 124–27: "Does any thoughtful man suppose that these tendencies will be eternal and that the present experiment in civilisation is the last the world will see?"

30. See *The Short Stories of F. Scott Fitzgerald*, ed. Matthew J. Bruccoli (New York: Charles Scribner's Sons, 1989), 512, 679, 277, 97–98, 194, 62–63, 237–38. Citations in my text are followed by page numbers.

31. See Beard and Beard, *Rise of American Civilization*, 2: 713ff.

32. Fitzgerald, *The Great Gatsby*, 31. William James, "The Varieties of Religious Experience," in *William James: Writings 1902–1910*, ed. Bruce Kuklick (New York: Library of America, 1987), 133. See Santayana, *Character and Opinion in the United States*, 107–10.

33. Lippmann, *Public Opinion*, 89–91.

34. C. Hugh Holman, "Fitzgerald's Changes on the Southern Belle: The Tarleton Trilogy," in *The Short Stories of F. Scott Fitzgerald: New Approaches in Criticism*, ed. Jackson R. Bryer (Madison: University of Wisconsin Press, 1982), 55.

35. Cleanth Brooks, *William Faulkner: Toward Yoknapatawpha and Beyond* (New Haven: Yale University Press, 1979), 272.

36. Beard and Beard, *Rise of American Civilization*, 2: 383–87.

37. F. Scott Fitzgerald, "Early Success," in *The Crack-Up*, ed. Edmund Wilson (New York: New Directions, 1956), 87.

38. Edith Wharton, *Edith Wharton: Novellas and Other Writings* (New York: Library of America, 1984), 781. See Barbara Sylvester, "Whose 'Babylon Revisited' Are We Teaching? Cowley's Fortunate Corruption—and Others Not So Fortunate," in *F. Scott Fitzgerald: New Perspectives*, ed. Jackson R. Breyer, Alan Margolies, and Ruth Prigozy (Athens: University of Georgia Press, 2000), 182–83 for analysis of the *Saturday Evening Post* text (1931) of the story, especially of the passage on "the great break between the generations ten or twelve years ago."

39. H. L. Mencken, *A Mencken Chrestomathy* (New York: Alfred A. Knopf, 1967), 183.

40. F. Scott Fitzgerald, *The Beautiful and Damned* (New York: Collier, 1986), 4. Citations in my text are followed by page numbers.

41. Fitzgerald, "Echoes of the Jazz Age," in *The Crack-Up*, 22.

42. See William James, "The Energies of Men," in *William James: Writings 1902–1910*, 1239.

43. See the discussion of James and the strenuous life in George Cotkin, *William*

James, Public Philosopher (Baltimore: Johns Hopkins University Press, 1990), 91–94. Cotkin makes a point relevant to the plot of Fitzgerald's *The Beautiful and Damned*: "The accumulation of wealth troubled Americans, in James's interpretation, no less than did their abject fears of losing whatever wealth they had accumulated."

44. James, "The Social Value of the College-Bred," in *William James, Public Philosopher*, 1245.

45. Horace M. Kallen, *Indecency and the Seven Arts* (New York: Horace Liveright, 1930), 3.

46. Lippmann, *Drift and Mastery*, 331–33.

47. John Dewey, "The Lost Individual," in *The Philosophy of John Dewey*, ed. John J. McDermott (Chicago: University of Chicago Press, 1981), 601, 605. Emphasis added.

48. Ibid., 598.

49. Fitzgerald, *The Great Gatsby*, 101. See Santayana, *Reason in Society*, 125: one hopes that a new civilization developed from our own "would be profounder than ours and more pervasive. But it doubtless cannot." Part of the problem is the herd mentality promoted by life in a commercial state—but, Santayana adds, we reject also the claims of "an aristocracy of wealth or power" which is definitively not "an aristocracy of noble minds" (132–33). Tom Buchanan plays out his themes in a dialogue considerably larger than he is.

Chapter 3

1. Edmund Wilson, *Letters on Literature and Politics, 1912–1972*, ed. Elena Wilson (New York: Farrar, Straus and Giroux, 1977); Jeffrey Meyers, *Edmund Wilson: A Biography* (Boston: Houghton Mifflin, 1995); Lewis M. Dabney, ed., *Edmund Wilson: Centennial Reflections* (Princeton: Princeton University Press, 1997); David Castronovo, *Edmund Wilson Revisited* (New York: Twayne, 1998); René Wellek, "Edmund Wilson (1895–1972)," in *History as a Tool in Critical Interpretation*, ed. Thomas F. Rugh and Erin R. Silva (Provo: Brigham Young University Press, 1978), 63–95.

2. See Frederick Copleston, S. J., *A History of Philosophy* (New York: Doubleday, 1994), 400, on the complexity of Whitehead's work.

3. Wellek, "Edmund Wilson (1895–1972)," 89.

4. Edmund Wilson, "The All-Star Literary Vaudeville" and "The Critic Who Does Not Exist," in *The Shores of Light: A Literary Chronicle of the Twenties and Thirties* (New York: Farrar, Straus and Young, 1952), 238, 369. See especially Wilson's defense of Whitehead in "Notes on Babbitt and More," 465.

5. Wilson, *Letters on Literature and Politics, 1912–1972*, 703.

6. Edmund Wilson, *From the Uncollected Edmund Wilson*, ed. Janet Groth and David Castronovo (Athens: Ohio University Press, 1995), 45–49.

7. Ibid., 47, 49. A few years later, in *Axel's Castle*, Wilson wrote that Valéry "was one of the first literary men to acquire a smattering of the new mathematical and physical theory. Valéry has, it is true, made interesting use of this, but one wishes sometimes

NOTES

that he would either go further with it or leave philosophy alone." Edmund Wilson, *Axel's Castle* (1931; reprint, New York: Charles Scribner's Sons, 1954), 79.

8. This low point of the narrator's mood is in Edmund Wilson, *I Thought of Daisy* (1929; reprint, Baltimore: Penguin, 1963), 126. Subsequent references are in my text.

9. Passages from Whitehead's *Modes of Thought* cited by Paul Grimley Kuntz, *Alfred North Whithead* (Boston: Twayne, 1984), 42–43.

10. Wilson, *Axel's Castle*, 119.

11. Wilson, "Modern Literature: Between the Whirlpool and the Rock," in *From the Uncollected Edmund Wilson,* 50: "Doctor Whitehead, in his *Science and the Modern World,* has suggested that the romantic movement of the early nineteenth century was, not merely a literary phenomenon, but really a philosophical reaction against the ideas of contemporary science. The mathematics of Descartes and Newton had their poetical equivalent in the exact and balanced couplets of Pope and the geometrical tragedies of Racine. And the poets, like the astronomers and physicists, had reduced the universe to an accurate machine obeying invariable natural laws."

12. Ibid., 52.

13. Ibid., 52–53.

14. Described at length in his (undated) letter to Maxwell Perkins sometime in September 1928, Wilson, *Letters on Literature and Politics, 1912–1972,* 149–51.

15. Wilson, "Modern Literature: Between the Whirlpool and the Rock," 54–55.

16. Ibid., 53–54.

17. Wilson, "A. N. Whitehead: Physicist and Prophet," in *From the Uncollected Edmund Wilson,* 62.

18. Ibid., 65–66.

19. Ibid., 67.

20. Ibid., 68–69.

21. Ibid., 71.

22. *Science and the Modern World* was published in 1925. Whitehead's work on symbolism began early in the century, was incorporated into *The Concept of Nature* (1920), and reappeared in the Barbour-Page Lectures at the University of Virginia in 1927. I cite the latter text.

23. Alfred North Whitehead, *Alfred North Whitehead: An Anthology,* ed. F. S. C. Northrop and Mason W. Gross (New York: MacMillan, 1953), 436–40.

24. Wilson, *Axel's Castle,* 157–58.

25. Whitehead, *Alfred North Whitehead: An Anthology,* 442–49.

26. See Sherman Paul, *Edmund Wilson: A Study of Literary Vocation in Our Time* (Urbana: University of Illinois Press, 1965), 53–65; James W. Tuttleton, "The Vexations of Modernism: Edmund Wilson's *Axel's Castle,*" *The American Scholar* (spring 1988): 264–65.

27. Sigmund Freud, *Civilization and Its Discontents,* ed. James Strachey (New York: W. W. Norton, 1961), 38–39. Freud stated that this was true of "the year 1930."

28. See Ronald Berman, *Fitzgerald, Hemingway, and the Twenties* (Tuscaloosa: University of Alabama Press, 2001), 11–27.

29. There is an enormous amount of Jamesian statement on the issue. See especially "The Will," in *The Principles of Psychology*, 2 vols., ed. Frederick H. Burkhardt (Cambridge: Harvard University Press, 1981), 2: 1167–70.

30. John Dewey, "Search for the Great Community," in *The Philosophy of John Dewey*, ed. John J. McDermott (Chicago: University of Chicago Press, 1981), 638.

31. Ibid., 611.

32. Whitehead, "Symbolism, Its Meaning and Effect," in *Alfred North Whitehead: An Anthology*, 534, 537.

33. Ibid., 540, 543–44, 546.

34. Whitehead, "The Romantic Reaction," in *Alfred North Whitehead: An Anthology*, 443, 447.

35. Whitehead, "Symbolism, Its Meaning and Effect," 534, 543.

36. Edmund Wilson, "Wellfleet and Stamford, 1949," in *The Forties*, ed. Leon Edel (New York: Farrar Straus and Giroux, 1984), 294.

37. William Hazlitt's *Lectures on English Philosophy* cited by David Bromwich, *Hazlitt: The Mind of a Critic* (New York: Oxford University Press, 1983), 27.

38. Whitehead, "The Romantic Reaction," 441.

39. Whitehead, "Symbolism, Its Meaning and Effect," 554–55.

40. Wilson, *I Thought of Daisy*, 147. Emphasis added.

41. Whitehead, "The Romantic Reaction," 433–42; "Symbolism," 534. See especially the long discussion of color, 540.

42. See Lionel Trilling, "Freud and Literature," in *The Liberal Imagination* (New York: Viking Press, 1950), 65.

Chapter 4

1. Harry Levin, "What Was Modernism?" in *Refractions: Essays in Comparative Literature* (New York: Oxford University Press, 1966), 271–95, especially 293–95. There is a discussion of William James's argument on the "rapid multiplication of theories" of truth. One consequence was a new belief about "the instability of language . . . and also . . . of the insufficiency of symbol" (302). See Gillian Beer's "Wave Theory and the Rise of Literary Modernism," in *Open Fields: Science in Cultural Encounter* (Oxford: Oxford University Press, 1999), 295–318.

2. Levin, "What Was Modernism?" in *Refractions*, 293–94.

3. Most visibly in the case of Josiah Royce, who consistently used poets and novelists as sources for case histories of "social experience." Royce was concerned essentially with the depiction of human relationship: friendship, guilt, love, and loyalty. See "Individual Experience and Social Experience" and "The Hope of the Great Community," in *The Basic Writings of Josiah Royce*, 2 vols., ed. John J. McDermott (Chicago: University of Chicago Press, 1969), 2: 1033–37, 1147. See also Ronald Berman, *The Great Gatsby and Fitzgerald's World of Ideas* (Tuscaloosa: University of Alabama Press, 1997), 155–61.

4. See Berman, *The Great Gatsby and Fitzgerald's World of Ideas*, 28–43; Ross Posnock, "The Influence of William James on American Culture," in *The Cambridge Companion to William James*, ed. Ruth Anna Putnam (Cambridge: Cambridge University Press, 1997), 322–42. Selections from James appeared frequently after his death. *The Will to Believe* was published in 1919, *Collected Essays* in 1920, *Some Problems of Philosophy* in 1921, *Talks to Teachers* in 1922, *The Varieties of Religious Experience* in 1923, the Modern Library edition of *The Philosophy of William James* in 1925, *An Alternative Use of Force* in 1926, *The Meaning of Truth* in 1927.

5. Harold E. Stearns, *Civilization in the United States* (London: Jonathan Cape, 1922), 152–53.

6. William James, *The Philosophy of William James*, ed. Horace M. Kallen (New York: The Modern Library, 1925), v. Emphasis added. See Charlene Haddock Seigfried, "James: Sympathetic Apprehension of the Point of View of the Other," in *Classical American Pragmatism*, ed. Sandra B. Rosenthal, Carl R. Hausman, and Douglas R. Anderson (Urbana: University of Illinois Press, 1999), 85–98.

7. James, *Philosophy of William James*, 9.

8. Ibid., 8–9.

9. James, "Talks to Teachers on Psychology," in *Philosophy of William James*, 280–82.

10. See Lionel Trilling, "Manners, Morals, and the Novel," in *The Liberal Imagination* (New York: Viking Press, 1950), 222: "For our time the most effective agent of the moral imagination has been the novel of the last two hundred years. It was never, either aesthetically or morally, a perfect form and its faults and failures can be quickly enumerated. But its greatness and its practical usefulness lay in its unremitting work of involving the reader himself in the moral life, inviting him to put his own motives under examination, suggesting that reality is not as his conventional education has led him to see it."

11. William James, *William James: Writings 1902–1910*, ed. Bruce Kuklick (New York: Library of America, 1987), 608, 1243–44.

12. Ibid., 690–710, especially 709.

13. Ibid., 731–55, especially 745–46.

14. John Dewey, *The Philosophy of John Dewey*, ed. John J. McDermott (Chicago: University of Chicago Press, 1981), 642–43. Like Royce, Dewey presents something of a problem. We might consider his evaluation—"an artist of the first order"—of W. H. Hudson ("The Live Creature and 'Etherial Things,'" 550). That would have been news to Hemingway, who devoted part of the opening of *The Sun Also Rises* to Hudson's destruction. See Alan Ryan, *John Dewey and the High Tide of American Liberalism* (New York: W. W. Norton, 1997), 92, 202, 265: Dewey's work on literature is, according to Ryan, "fuzzy-edged" and "sometimes labored," but immensely insightful.

15. Dewey, "The Live Creature and 'Etherial Things,'" in *Philosophy of John Dewey*, 550–51.

16. Dewey, "Existence, Value and Criticism," in *Philosophy of John Dewey*, 335.

17. Ryan, *John Dewey and the High Tide of American Liberalism*, 128. See James, "Concerning Fechner," *William James: Writings 1902–1910*, 698: without an appropriate language, "the book of nature turns into a volume on mechanics, in which whatever has life is treated as a sort of anomaly."

18. Ryan, *John Dewey and the High Tide of American Liberalism*, 188–89.

19. Ibid., 104.

20. Robert B. Westbrook, *John Dewey and American Democracy* (Ithaca: Cornell University Press, 1991), 336–37.

21. See Horace M. Kallen in *Indecency and the Seven Arts* (New York: Horace Liveright, 1930), 145: "There exists no word with a meaning explicit, specific, and tangible. Meanings are as subtle fluids. Words are like barren stream-beds into and out of which the meanings are continuously flowing, stirring them to fruitfulness and life. All words, consequently, are ambiguous. . . . The import of things lies in what relations they bear to other things."

22. Edmund Wilson, *Axel's Castle* (1931; reprint, New York: Charles Scribner's Sons, 1954), 1–25, especially 3, 5.

23. Ibid., 21.

24. Ibid., 75.

25. Ibid., 284.

26. Edmund Wilson, *The Twenties*, ed. Leon Edel (New York: Farrar, Straus and Giroux, 1975), 249.

27. Ibid., 312.

28. Edmund Wilson, *I Thought of Daisy* (1929; reprint, Baltimore: Penguin Books, 1963), 133.

29. Edward O. Wilson, *Consilience* (New York: Vintage, 1998), 234–35.

30. Ibid., 66. The weakest part of the idea of "consilience" is its primitive understanding of fiction. It assumes that myth and folk tales constitute literature, although they are only its matrix. The theory leaves out language.

31. Lionel Trilling, *Mind in the Modern World* (New York: Viking, 1972), 35.

32. Lionel Trilling, *Sincerity and Authenticity* (Cambridge: Harvard University Press, 1971), 76–80.

33. Edmund Wilson, *The Twenties*, 350–53.

34. Ibid., 428.

35. Ibid., 421–27. See especially Wilson's discussion (351) of Proust arguing for "qualities or tendencies" or even for "his own desires." See also Gillian Beer, "Wave Theory and the Rise of Literary Modernism," *Open Fields*, 295: the "late 1920s and 1930s" are the optimum period in which to study science on the impossibility of formulating reality. It was much argued in that period, with reference to Eddington and Einstein, that "realism" could never be more than an approximation of reality.

36. Lionel Trilling, "Art, Will, and Necessity," in *The Last Decade* (New York: Harcourt Brace Jovanovich, 1979), 145–46.

37. Lionel Trilling, *Matthew Arnold* (New York: Harcourt Brace Jovanovich, 1977), 83.

38. Ibid., 102.

39. Ibid., 348–49.

40. Ibid., 356–57. See 324–31, 363–64.

41. Trilling, "Manners, Morals, and the Novel," 212–13.

42. Ibid., 215.

43. Lionel Trilling, "Hemingway and His Critics," in *Speaking of Literature and Society* (New York: Harcourt Brace Jovanovich, 1980), 125.

44. Trilling, "Manners, Morals and the Novel," 215–16. See Beer, "Wave Theory and the Rise of Literary Modernism," 306–15 for the description of James Clerk Maxwell's work on the "obduracies of the invisible material world" and of John Tyndall's engagement with alternate "narratives" of the nature of reality.

45. Lionel Trilling, "F. Scott Fitzgerald," in *The Liberal Imagination*, 245–49.

46. Trilling, "Reality in America," in *The Liberal Imagination*, 12–13.

47. Trilling, "Freud and Literature," in *The Liberal Imagination*, 40–41.

48. Trilling, "The Princess Casamassima," in *The Liberal Imagination*, 65.

CHAPTER 5

1. From Bertrand Russell's Introduction to Ludwig Wittgenstein's *Tractatus Logico-Philosophicus* (1922; reprint, Mineola, N.Y.: Dover, 1999), 8.

2. Bertrand Russell, *My Philosophical Development* (New York: Simon and Schuster, 1959), 13–14. The argument that men should deliver "so many *things*, almost in an equal number or *words*" has a long history: see Thomas Sprat, *The History of the Royal Society* (St. Louis: Washington University Press, 1966), 112–13.

3. See Ronald Berman, *Fitzgerald, Hemingway, and the Twenties* (Tuscaloosa: University of Alabama Press, 2001), 116–41.

4. Ludwig Wittgenstein, *Culture and Value,* ed. G. H. Von Wright (Chicago: University of Chicago Press, 1984), 7e–8e. For a recent study of meaning in experience see Avrum Stroll, *Moore and Wittgenstein on Certainty* (New York: Oxford University Press, 1994), 126–34.

5. Ernest Hemingway, *The Sun Also Rises* (1926; reprint, New York: Charles Scribner's Sons, 1970), 245. All future references to this edition are in parentheses in my text.

6. Donald Davidson, "Truth and Meaning," in *Perspectives in the Philosophy of Language* (Toronto: Broadview, 2000), 83. Davidson cites Alfred Tarski. See the elegant discussion by Jane Austen in chapter 18 of *Sense and Sensibility:* "I have kept my feelings to myself, because I could find no language to describe them." *The Novels of Jane Austen,* ed. R. W. Chapman, 5 vols. (Oxford: Oxford University Press, 1967), 1: 96–98.

7. Davidson, "Truth and Meaning," 83.

8. This passage from Henri Bergson's *Time and Free Will: An Essay on the Immediate Data of Consciousness* (1910) is cited by Louis Menand in *Discovering Modernism: T. S. Eliot and His Context* (New York: Oxford University Press, 1988), 35.

9. Russell was of course more subtle and should be given credit for his toleration and even support of the Wittgenstein view.

10. Louis Sass, "Deep Disquietudes: Reflections on Wittgenstein as Antiphilosopher," in *Wittgenstein: Biography and Philosophy,* ed. James C. Klagge (Cambridge: Cambridge University Press, 2001), 131–33. See also Isaiah Berlin's essay "The Sense of Reality" in his book with that title (New York: Farrar, Straus and Giroux, 1998), 1–39. See especially Berlin's discussion of the intellectual refusal to state more than can be true (27).

11. Ernest Hemingway, *A Moveable Feast* (New York: Charles Scribner's Sons, 1964), 5–6.

12. Ernest Hemingway, "Monologue to the Maestro: A High Seas Letter," in *By-Line: Ernest Hemingway* (New York: Touchstone, 1998), 216.

13. John Dewey, "Existence, Value and Criticism," in *The Later Works, 1925–1953,* 2 vols., ed. Jo Ann Boydston (Carbondale: Southern Illinois University Press, 1981), 1: 304–5. See Raymond D. Boisvert, *John Dewey: Rethinking Our Time* (Albany: State University Press of New York, 1998), 122–35; also Philip W. Jackson, *John Dewey and the Lessons of Art* (New Haven: Yale University Press, 1998), 121–30.

14. Alfred North Whitehead, "Adventures of Ideas," in *Alfred North Whitehead: An Anthology,* ed. F. S. C. Northrop and Mason W. Gross (New York: Macmillan, 1953), 846. "Adventures of Ideas" appeared in 1933, but the editors note that these essays are developments of Whitehead's previous work. See Robert Spaemann, "Which Experiences Teach Us to Understand the World," in *Whitehead's Metaphysics of Creativity* (Albany: State University of New York Press, 1990), 154.

15. See Edward F. Stanton, *Hemingway and Spain* (Seattle: University of Washington Press, 1989), 132–39.

16. There are connections between the sixth chapter of *The Sun Also Rises* and the sixteenth chapter of Harold Stearns's autobiography. See *The Confessions of a Harvard Man* (Sutton West, Ont., and Santa Barbara, Calif.: Paget Press, 1984), 297–99. Originally published in 1935 as *The Street I Know*. Stearns's chapter discusses Hemingway and other writers in Paris in the twenties. Like Frances (Robert Cohn's mistress), Stearns sees through the lofty argument of going to Paris for the sake of "literature." like Jake Barnes, who is worried about the transformation of Cohn's "healthy conceit" to something much worse, Stearns understands that expatriate ambition necessarily ends in "arrogance." Like Hemingway himself, Stearns believes that most Americans in Paris are incompetents. They may well begin in "wishing and dreaming" but often end in fistfights over empty ideals.

17. See Elizabeth Dewberry, "Hemingway's Journalism and the Realist Dilemma,"

in *The Cambridge Companion to Ernest Hemingway,* ed. Scott Donaldson (Cambridge: Cambridge University Press, 1996), 23–29.

18. Ernest Hemingway, *A Farewell to Arms* (1929; reprint, New York: Charles Scribner's Sons, 1969), 27.

19. Dewberry, "Hemingway's Journalism and the Realist Dilemma," 29. See Nancy Franklin, "The Theatre," *New Yorker,* November 27, 2000, 179: "In a speech that Pinter gave at a student drama festival in 1962, he discussed the 'highly ambiguous business' of language: 'You and I, the characters which grow on a page, most of the time we're inexpressive, giving little away, unreliable, elusive, evasive, obstructive, unwilling. But it's out of these attributes that a language arises. A language . . . where under what is said, another thing is being said.'"

20. Alfred North Whitehead, "Science and the Modern World," in *Alfred North Whitehead: An Anthology,* 459. Emphasis added. See Gerald E. Myers, *William James: His Life and Thought* (New Haven: Yale University Press, 1986), 144–47, 337.

Chapter 6

1. Ernest Hemingway, *Ernest Hemingway: Selected Letters, 1917–1961,* ed. Carlos Baker (New York: Charles Scribner's Sons, 1981), 354, 363, 375.

2. See for example John Leonard, "'A Man of The World' and 'A Clean, Well-Lighted Place': "Hemingway's Unified View of Old Age," *Hemingway Review* 13, no. 2 (spring 1994): 62–73.

3. See R. L. Colie, "Some Paradoxes in the Language of Things," in *Reason and the Imagination: Studies in the History of Ideas, 1600–1800,* ed. J. A. Mazzeo (New York: Columbia University Press, 1962), 93–128.

4. Ernest Hemingway, "A Clean, Well-Lighted Place," in *Ernest Hemingway: The Short Stories* (New York: Scribner, 1995), 382 (subsequent references are in my text); "Now I Lay Me," in *Ernest Hemingway: The Short Stories,* 367.

5. See Michael Reynolds's discussion of the religious context of *The Sun Also Rises* in *Hemingway: The Paris Years* (Oxford: Basil Blackwell, 1990), 325–27.

6. See the extensive citation of these subjects by Louis L. Martz, *The Poetry of Meditation* (New Haven: Yale University Press, 1954), 179–210, especially 206–9. See also 129: "When an agreeable object is presented to the senses, do not become absorbed in its material elements, but let the understanding judge it."

7. According to the *Oxford English Dictionary.*

8. Martz, *The Poetry of Meditation,* 207.

9. Ibid., 208.

10. This citation from Paul Tillich's *The Protestant Era* is from Ronald Berman, "Herrick's Secular Poetry," in *Ben Jonson and the Cavalier Poets,* ed. Hugh Maclean (New York: W. W. Norton, 1974), 537.

11. See Sheldon Norman Grebstein, "Hemingway's Dialogue," in *Hemingway's*

Craft (Carbondale: Southern Illinois University Press, 1973), 99: "It is as though the reader were presented with a bare scenario which retained only the actor's speeches, and asked to do the work of writer and director in order to reconstruct the scene fully and dramatize it."

12. See Joseph M. Flora, *Ernest Hemingway: A Study of the Short Fiction* (Boston: Twayne, 1989), 20: "The simple vocabulary of the story and the simple structure of the sentences are in keeping with the parable-like effect of the story. The rhythms of the King James Bible were a powerful influence on Hemingway's style, and that rhythm is especially appropriate to this story about longing for spiritual meaning." Flora adds that the old man is "an allegorical figure."

13. See discussion of "The still moment of time—the moment in which human beings make decisions" by Earl Rovit and Gerry Brenner, *Ernest Hemingway* (Boston: Twayne, 1986), 95.

14. See Francis Bacon, *Essays, Advancement of Learning, New Atlantis, and Other Pieces*, ed. Richard Foster Jones (New York: Odyssey Press, 1937), 122–24.

15. John Earle, *Microcosmography*, ed. Alfred S. West (Cambridge: Cambridge University Press, 1951), 3. Earle describes approximately seventy different forms of "character." See also Jean de la Bruyère, "Of Mankind," in *The Characters of Jean de la Bruyère*, trans. Henri van Laun (London: George Routledge and Sons Ltd., 1929), 271–327. There is an analysis of modern subjectivity in "Demotic Life and Times" by Jacques Barzun, *From Dawn to Decadence* (New York: HarperCollins, 2000), 773–802.

16. See Jeremy Taylor, *The Rule and Exercises of Holy Dying* (London: William Pickering, 1847), 9, on age as exemplar: "Death meets us everywhere."

17. Robert Herrick, "Divination by a Daffadil," in *The Poems of Robert Herrick*, ed. L. C. Martin (Oxford: Oxford University Press, 1965), 38.

18. Alfred Alvarez, *The School of Donne* (New York: Pantheon, 1961), 12–14. See the exhaustive treatment of medieval and seventeenth-century texts that may have been on Hemingway's mind by H. R. Stoneback, "'Lovers' Sonnets Turn'd to Holy Psalms': The Soul's Song of Providence, the Scandal of Suffering, and Love in *A Farewell to Arms*," *Hemingway Review* 9, no. 1 (fall 1989): 33–76; especially discussion of "initiations" and "symbolic landscape" in *A Farewell To Arms* (70).

19. H. E. Bates, "Hemingway's Short Stories," in *Hemingway and His Critics*, ed. Carlos Baker (New York: Hill and Wang, 1961), 77 (Bates cites the phrase "living people" from the "ice-berg" passage of *Death in the Afternoon*).

20. Ibid., 76. Bates's ironies are not fully under control, so it is hard to know if that is his opinion or an opinion being challenged.

21. Ernest Hemingway, "Monologue to the Maestro: A High Seas Letter," in *By-Line: Ernest Hemingway*, ed. William White (New York: Touchstone, 1998), 219. Questioning and understanding are important ideas—and terms—in Hemingway. See note number 6.

22. Alfred North Whitehead, "The Romantic Reaction," from *Science and the*

Modern World, in *Alfred North Whitehead: An Anthology,* ed. F. S. C. Northrop and Mason W. Gross (New York: Macmillan, 1953), 439. Edmund Wilson read this essay when it came out, and referred to it a number of times: see "A. N. Whitehead and Bertrand Russell," in *From the Uncollected Edmund Wilson,* ed. Janet Groth and David Castronovo (Athens: Ohio University Press, 1995), 45–49; "A. N. Whitehead: Physicist and Prophet," 56–72; *Axel's Castle* (1931; reprint, New York: Charles Scribner's Sons, 1954), 5–6. It is fair to say that this part of *Science and the Modern World* influenced him and those whom he influenced.

23. Whitehead, "The Romantic Reaction," 443.

24. Harry Levin, "Observations on the Style of Ernest Hemingway," in *Hemingway and His Critics,* 112. Levin uses the idea of correspondences in a different sense from the seventeenth-century writers I have cited. He does not mean that a reference, say, to the sun, is also a reference to a king, but that language must refer adequately to observed fact.

25. T. S. Eliot, "Lancelot Andrewes," in *Selected Essays* (New York: Harcourt, Brace, 1950), 305.

26. John Dewey, "Experience and Thinking," in *The Philosophy of John Dewey,* ed. John J. McDermott (Chicago: University of Chicago Press, 1981), 494–99.

27. Cited by Marjorie Perloff in *Wittgenstein's Ladder* (Chicago: University of Chicago Press, 1996), 62; Ludwig Wittgenstein, *Culture and Value,* ed. G. H. Von Wright (Chicago: University of Chicago Press, 1984), 7e–8e. Isaiah Berlin writes of displaced Cartesian certainties that had insisted "that if the human mind can be cleared of dogma, prejudice and cant, of the organised obscurities and Aristotelian patter of the schoolmen, then nature will at last be seen in the full symmetry and harmony of its elements, which can be described, analysed and represented by a logically appropriate language." In "The Sciences and The Humanities," in *Against the Current* (New York: Viking, 1980), 83.

28. Jackson J. Benson stated in 1989 that he had read "seventeen articles devoted to this subject" and that "further articles are in the works." See his "Criticism of the Short Stories: The Neglected and the Oversaturated—An Editorial," *Hemingway Review* 8, no. 2 (spring 1989): 31–32. See also Paul Smith, "A Note on a New Manuscript of 'A Clean, Well-Lighted Place,'" 36–39, which cites the textual history. See especially the essay by Warren Bennett cited in my following note.

29. Warren Bennett, "The Characterization and the Dialogue Problem in Hemingway's 'A Clean, Well-Lighted Place,'" *Hemingway Review* 9, no. 2 (spring 1990): 94–123, especially 119.

30. Isaiah Berlin, *The Sense of Reality* (New York: Farrar, Straus and Giroux, 1998), 170–74.

31. "Everyman," in *The Genius of the Early English Theater,* ed. Sylvan Barnet, Morton Berman, and William Burto (New York: New American Library, 1962), 82; John Bunyan, *The Pilgrim's Progress* (London: J. M. Dent and Sons, 1961), 143–48.

32. See Carlos Baker, *Hemingway: The Writer as Artist* (Princeton: Princeton University Press, 1973), 123–24; Flora, *Ernest Hemingway: A Study of the Short Fiction*, 24–25.

33. Ernest Hemingway, *A Farewell to Arms* (1929; reprint, New York: Scribner, 1957), 261.

34. See the discussion of "influence" and of "clear affinities" between ideas by Hans-Johann Glock, "Wittgenstein and Reasoning," in *Wittgenstein: Biography and Philosophy*, ed. James C. Klagge (Cambridge: Cambridge University Press, 2001), 198–203.

35. Ludwig Wittgenstein, *Tractatus Logico-Philosophicus* (1922; reprint, Mineola, N.Y.: Dover Publications, 1999), 107. From passages 6.5 and 6.52.

36. Russell, in his Introduction to the edition of the *Tractatus* above cited, 22.

37. See Louis Sass, "Deep Disquietudes: Reflections on Wittgenstein as Antiphilosopher," in *Wittgenstein: Biography and Philosophy*, 100. The essay cites *Recollections of Wittgenstein*, in which the philosopher responded to his sister Hermine about the possibility of her knowing *anything* about his state of mind: "You remind me of somebody who is looking out through a closed window and cannot explain to himself the strange movements of a passer-by. He cannot tell what sort of storm is raging out there or that this person might only be managing with difficulty to stay on his feet." In regard to this point, Hemingway wrote in the early thirties that he was "trying, always, to convey to the reader a full and complete feeling" of his own experience. However, "because it is very hard to do I must sometimes fail." From an undated letter intended to be sent out to his readers in *The Only Thing That Counts: The Ernest Hemingway/Maxwell Perkins Correspondence, 1925–1947*, ed. Matthew J. Bruccoli (Columbia: University of South Carolina Press, 1996), 180.

38. See John Dewey's early twenties essay on "the flickering inconsequential acts of separate selves" in "Morality is Social," in *Philosophy of John Dewey*, ed. John J. McDermott, 713–18.

39. This passage from Alfred North Whitehead's *The Aims of Education* cited by Paul Grimley Kuntz in *Alfred North Whitehead* (Boston: Twayne, 1984), 29.

INDEX

Abrams, M. H., 19, 20, 21
Alvarez, Alfred, 90

Babbitt, George, 3, 25
Babbitt, Irving, 11, 24, 29
Bacon, Sir Francis, 89
Bates, H. E., 90–91
Beard, Charles A. and Mary R., 25–26, 35
Beer, Gillian, 112n. 35
Bennett, Warren, 94
Bergson, Henri, 77
Berlin, Isaiah: Cartesian certainties, 117n. 27; definitions of romanticism, 9; myth of progress, 22; neglect of art, 15–16; questions, 94–95
Bishop, John Peale, 2
Brooks, Cleanth, 35
Brooks, Van Wyck: *American Civilization,* 28; *America's Coming-of-Age,* 29; John Dewey, 10; Ralph Waldo Emerson, 10; William James, 10
Butler, Marilyn, 15

civilization: body politic, 38–40; energies, 37–40; progress, 36
Civilization in the United States, 28, 31, 59
Coleridge, Samuel Taylor, 20

Davidson, Donald, 77
Dewey, John: anxiety, 39–40; experience, 55, 79; W. H. Hudson, 79, 111n. 14;

Dewey, John (*continued*)
  language, 1, 93; Walter Pater, 64; philosophy, 6, 79; presentation, 63; "Search for the Great Community," 63–64; "Towards a New Individualism," 51; Alfred North Whitehead, 47; William Wordsworth, 65
Dos Passos, John, 86

Edel, Leon, 66, 68
Eliot, T. S., 11; Lancelot Andrewes, 93; language, 93; literary history, 90
Everyman, 89, 95

Fairchild, Hoxie, 15
Fitzgerald, F. Scott: Sherwood Anderson, 12; "Babylon Revisited," 34; *The Beautiful and Damned*, 31, 36–38; Peggy Boyd, 17; Thomas Boyd, 13, 19, 20; civilization, 3, 14; Joseph Conrad, 12, 20–21; criticism, 1–3; Floyd Dell, 13; John Dos Passos, 13; Theodore Dreiser, 13; "The Diamond as Big as the Ritz," 26, 32, 33; "Dice, Brassknuckles & Guitar," 32; "Early Success," 18; *A Farewell to Arms*, 2; *The Great Gatsby*, 11, 15, 17–18, 19, 21–22, 25, 27, 29, 32, 33, 40–41, 50; Zane Grey, 13; "Handle With Care," 15; heightened perception, 2–3; "How to Waste Material," 19, 23; Rupert Hughes, 13; Aldous Huxley, 16–17; "The Ice Palace," 33–35; "The Jelly-Bean," 32; John Keats, 9; *Main Street*, 13; "May Day," 32; Charles Norris, 16; "The Offshore Pirate," 18; Oxford, 14; "Rags Martin-Jones and The PR-NCE of W-LES," 32; realism, 14–15; romantic limits, 17; romantic sentiment, 20; Rome, 14; *The Sheik*, 13; "The Swimmers," 32; Booth Tarkington, 13; *Ulysses*, 12; "Winter Dreams," 21
Fitzgerald, Zelda, 31
Freud, Sigmund: civilization, 26; *Civilization and Its Discontents*, 29; technology, 50

Gauss, Christian, 49
Goethe, Johann Wolfgang von, 20
Grant, Madison, 27
Grenburg, Bruce L., 104n. 28

Haggard, H. Rider, 29–30
Hartman, Geoffrey H., 11
Hazlitt, William, 54
Hemingway, Ernest: "A Clean, Well-Lighted Place," 86–100; allegory, 89, 97; *A Farewell to Arms*, 7, 81; "Indian Camp," 95; interpretation, 81–82; language, 7–8, 77, 91–93; H. L. Mencken, 80; perception, 78; re-

INDEX

ality, 8; self, 99; subjectivity, 99; *The Sun Also Rises,* 7, 8, 76–78, 80–85; time, 87–88

Herrick, Robert, 89–90

James, William: absolute present, 34; "Bergson and Intellectualism," 62; "The Compounding of Consciousness," 62; "Concerning Fechner," 62; Charles Darwin, 60–61; drift, 50; "Is Life Worth Living?" 38; literature, 9–10; *The Philosophy of William James,* 59–60; *A Pluralistic Universe,* 62; *Pragmatism,* 10, 61–62; reality, 62–63; "The Social Value of the College-Bred," 61; vitality, 37–38; Walt Whitman, 10, 61–62

Jersey City Evening Journal, 17

Kallen, Horace M.: body politic, 38; William James, 59–60; language, 112n. 21

Keats, John, 21

Leibniz, Gottfried Wilhelm, 45

Leslie, Shane, 17

Levin, Harry, 58–59, 92–93

Lippmann, Walter: American literature, 6; civilization, 27; *Drift and Mastery,* 38–39; experience, 2, 6; past and present, 36; Upton Sinclair, 5, 7; social time, 34

Lovejoy, A. O., 9

Lowie, Robert H., 59

Mencken, H. L.: American Literature, 9; mass man, 36; Friedrich Nietzsche, 17–19; *Prejudices: Second Series,* 28; "The Sahara of the Bozart," 28

metaphysical poetry, 87

Moore, Marianne, 73, 79

More, Paul Elmer, 10–11, 24

New Republic, 47

New York World, 31

Overton, Grant, 29

The Pilgrim's Progress, 95

Pinter, Harold, 115n. 19

Romaine, Paul, 86

romanticism: critical thought, 23; exact detail, 20; imagination, 14;

romanticism (*continued*)
    necessity, 102–3n. 4; objectivity, 14; reality, 19; renewal, 19–20; self, 15; suddenness, 20; youth, 23
Royce, Josiah, 5, 110n. 3
Russell, Bertrand: language, 7, 75, 76
Ryan, Alan, 64–65

St. Paul Daily News, 13
Santayana, George: *Character and Opinion in the United States,* 28; civilization, 31–32, 107n. 29, 108n. 49; language, 7; light, 8; perception, 5
Sass, Louis, 78
Saturday Evening Post, 3
Scribner's Magazine, 86
Shelley, Percy Bysshe, 4, 45, 46, 48
Smith, Norman Kemp, 46–47
Spengler, Oswald, 29, 31
Stearns, Harold E., 28, 31, 80
Stendhal (Marie-Henri Beyle), 82
Stern, Milton R., 22
Stoddard, Lothrop, 27, 29
Stoneback, H. R., 116n. 18
symbolism, 45–46, 51–57

Tillich, Paul, 88
Trilling, Lionel: Honoré de Balzac, 70; Theodore Dreiser, 70; experience, 6; extradition, 69; F. Scott Fitzgerald, 23–24, 72–73; Sigmund Freud, 73; Ernest Hemingway, 6–7; "Hemingway and His Critics," 71–72; Henry James, 70; William James, 69–70; *The Liberal Imagination,* 1; "Manners, Morals, and the Novel," 70, 72; *Mansfield Park,* 68; *Matthew Arnold,* 69; Marianne Moore, 73; "The Princess Casamassima," 73; reality, 70, 71, 72, 111n. 10

Van Loon, Hendrik Willem, 27

Wasserman, Earl, 14
Wellek, René, 23, 42, 47
Wharton, Edith, 36
Whitehead, Alfred North: civilization, 29; language, 79; perception, 5, 91–92; philosophy, 42–57; *Science and the Modern World,* 4, 48, 55; Percy Bysshe Shelley, 4, 45, 46, 48; specious present, 82; symbolism, 51–57; William Wordsworth, 4, 45, 46, 48, 91–92

INDEX

Wilson, Edmund: *Axel's Castle*, 4, 45, 48, 65–66; Van Wyck Brooks, 43; civilization, 27–28; Albert Einstein, 43, 47; T. S. Eliot, 43, 69; experience, 67; *The Forties*, 54; *I Thought of Daisy*, 4, 5, 30, 44, 48–51; language, 66; H. L. Mencken, 43; John Milton, 11; Paul Elmer More, 43; Marcel Proust, 47; reality, 6; romanticism, 4, 11–12; Bertrand Russell, 43–44; *Science and the Modern World*, 43–48, 52, 53, 55; symbolism, 51–57; Henry David Thoreau, 29; *The Twenties*, 67–68; Paul Valéry, 44, 47, 65; Alfred North Whitehead, 42–57, 109n. 11; *The Wound and the Bow*, 67

Wilson, Edward O., 67–68

Wittgenstein, Ludwig: knowledge, 118n. 37; language, 75–77, 94; progress, 30; questions, 98; talk, 78

Wordsworth, William, 15, 20, 21, 52, 58–59, 65